PARANORMAL COZY MYSTERY

Wakes & High Stakes

TRIXIE SILVERTALE

Sittin' On A Goldmine
Productions L.L.C.

Sittin' On A Goldmine Productions, L.L.C.

info@sittinonagoldmine.co

www.sittinonagoldmine.co

Publisher's note: This is a work of fiction. Names, characters, places and incidents are products of the author's imagination or are used fictitiously and are not to be construed as real. Any resemblance to actual events, locales, organizations, or persons, living or dead, is entirely coincidental.

ISBN: 978-1-952739-11-8

Cover Design © Sittin' On A Goldmine Productions, L.L.C.

Trixie Silvertale
Wakes and High Stakes: Paranormal Cozy Mystery : a novel / by Trixie Silvertale — 1st ed.
[1. Paranormal Cozy Mystery — Fiction. 2. Cozy Mystery — Fiction. 3. Amateur Sleuths — Fiction. 4. Female Sleuth — Fiction. 5. Wit and Humor — Fiction.] 1. Title.

CHAPTER 1

I'VE SEEN MORE than my share of dead bodies since arriving in Pin Cherry Harbor, but there's something different about this one. First of all, it's in a casket, and, secondly, I'm not being accused of putting it there.

It's also worth mentioning that I never met the deceased. She ran in the same upper-echelon of Pin Cherry society as my grandmother, so my father and I were invited purely as a sign of status. Ew. Attempting to hurry past the expertly coiffed corpse of Liliané Barnes, festooned with garish diamond brooches, earrings, and several massive rings, something catches my eye. I pause for a moment and stare at the inexplicable holes in this jet setter's over-priced lapel.

Hmmmm. I chew the inside of my cheek. Two

pin-prick-sized holes, about a finger's width apart. An unusual blemish in an otherwise spotless cosmic-cobalt designer suit.

My father gently tugs my sleeve, and I follow him back to our seats in the quaint, musty chapel hosting the viewing.

While we wait for the line of mourners to thin down, my mind drifts to memories of my dearly departed mother. She was young, radiant, and full of life. No matter how much time passes, I can never understand why she was taken from me when I was so young. As I struggle to access any recollection of her funeral, I'm disturbed by the black void where those heartbreaking images should be.

It seems natural to me that the memory of her face is fuzzy, since no pictures of her survived my six-year stint in foster care. And I can even accept that the sound of her voice is fading with time, but why can't I remember her funeral?

Sadly, she died in a horrible commuter-train-versus-automobile accident, so it certainly would've been closed casket, but I can't recall a single detail.

No casket.

No chapel.

No tears over an open grave as they lowered her—

"Mitzy? Mitzy?" My father taps my knee and stares at me with growing concern. "Did you slip away into one of those, what do you call 'em, inside pictures?"

My throat is tight with unwelcome emotion. "I can't really talk about it."

An ache of regret knifes through his eyes. "I'm so sorry I wasn't there for you."

I nod soberly and retreat back into my painful nostalgia. No one can blame him for not being there. He and my mother were a one-night stand, and she never bothered to track down the handsome out-of-towner who left her with much more than a warm memory of some Greek cheese. She happily named me after the dairy product that featured prominently in their "meet-cute," raised me on her own, and never said an unkind word about my biological father. In fact, she never spoke about him at all. To the point when, I eventually believed he must've died. When the Grim Reaper truly visited the Moon household and took my mom, it came as no actual surprise to find myself in and out of foster homes for the next few years.

It wasn't until I reached the ripe old age of seventeen that I successfully emancipated myself from the school of hard knocks. And by emancipated I mean ran away, and by successful I mean a series of dead-end jobs eking out a living on minimum wage.

Imagine my shock and disbelief when a frumpy man with an unbelievably enormous mustache showed up at the door of my should-be-condemned studio apartment in Sedona, Arizona, and handed me a manila envelope containing more hope than I ever dared wish for.

A lengthy journey, on a bus bursting with unpleasant odors, landed me in almost-Canada, and the moment I stepped onto the curb in Pin Cherry Harbor—my drab sepia-tone world exploded into Technicolor.

I lean toward my anxious father and whisper, "Maybe we can head over to the diner and get a proper breakfast after this. I'm not sure how much longer I'll survive on a handful of Fruity Puffs."

My suggestion brings a smile of relief to his face and a spark of hope to his grey eyes. "Sure. We should talk."

I work hard to maintain a protective wall around my heart. On the outside, I nod pleasantly, but on the inside, the tightening in my chest confirms that I'm not eager to delve into mucky emotional territory. Keeping things easy breezy has pretty much been my trick to survival all these years.

The pencil-thin wisp of a funeral director gently calls the room to order as the last stragglers return to their seats.

"Friends and relatives of Liliané Barnes, welcome to the Chapel of Eternal Rest. The family appreciates your outpouring of sympathy and condolences. Liliané's oldest daughter, Iris, would like to say a few words." His voice is light and airy. It's a version of Bob Ross, the happy painter, but with even less conviction. The man waves one of his oddly long arms toward a woman in the front row. He resembles a stick figure come to life.

The woman we've been told is Iris—severe bleached-blonde bob, late thirties, all angles—approaches the small podium, but her dark eyes are not rimmed with tears. Her sharp beak of a nose twitches once before she begins. "The family thanks you for coming."

When she grips the edges of the wooden rostrum, I notice her surprisingly short fingernails. I would've expected her to have a perfect French-tipped manicure. Maybe the stress of losing her mother caused her to bite them to the quick?

"As most of you know, my sister, brother, and I have maintained rooms at the manor, despite being estranged from my globe-trotting mother for some time. We came to pay our respects, for what that's worth. But I won't stand up here and pretend to be sad." Her crisp voice bears a shocking lack of emotion. "Lillian was a fairly horrible woman and I refuse to manufacture emotions that don't exist. I appreciate the kind words, but there's no need to feel pity for me. I'm not upset."

And with that, Iris holds her arrow-like chin high and returns to the empty seat next to her frowning, thinning-on-top husband.

Well, she's clearly not stressed. I also notice that Iris used her mother's given name, Lillian, and did not adopt the recent change in pronunciation made by the addition of an "e" with the accent *aigu*. Which, according to my sources, returned with the deceased from Europe three years ago. There was the "e," the accent mark, and husband number nine.

My mouth is hanging open like the clown hazard on a miniature golf course. Having my mom ripped from my life more than a decade ago broke me in ways I can't even explain. To sit here and listen to a woman who appears to have no regrets over losing her own mother does not compute. I struggle to close my gaping maw and make sense of what I've just heard.

The funeral director returns to the front of the room and faintly calls the son. "Roman, would you care to share a memory?"

A redheaded man in his early thirties, with well-groomed facial hair, shakes his head vigorously.

Apparently, this Prince Harry lookalike isn't even willing to make a hollow effort.

The oddly frail mortician swallows awkwardly

and attempts to draw the middle child, Violet, from her seat.

Despite his nearly inaudible urgings, she shakes her brooding brunette ponytail, but her refusal seems to come from a place of emotional over-whelm. She's weeping dramatically into a handker-chief and at least appears to mourn her mother's passing.

The magic mood ring I inherited from my grandmother sizzles with heat on my left hand and I glance down in time to see a flash of the Acropolis. I have no idea what this psychic information means, but my ever-expanding extra senses do pick up on some genuine sadness coming from Violet.

I suppose I should mention, in addition to an amazing bookshop, a vast financial estate, and a spoiled rotten caracal who eats children's cereal, I also inherited some inexplicable psychic gifts from my late grandmother.

Another name is murmured, and a darkly hand-some man, also in his early thirties, approaches the podium. He's not much taller than me, but his swagger commands attention. He has the kind of "bad boy" vibe that would've had me tripping over my own tongue to buy him a drink, back in the des-perate days before I met the local sheriff.

His black hair hangs in loose waves and he's dressed in a tailored Armani suit that screams money. As he spins the tale of his magical meeting with Liliané in Greece, the message from my ring becomes clear.

This man, thirty-some years younger than the deceased, is the latest in her long line of *former* husbands.

His voice is thick with emotion and he encourages us all to remember Liliané as the generous philanthropist she was. "Thank you all for coming, and I look forward to seeing more of our special guests this evening aboard the *Jewel of the Harbor*."

My eyes dart to my dad. "You're still going to that? Right?"

He chuckles. "After your grandmother spent weeks designing your custom dress? I wouldn't dare miss it."

I put a hand over my mouth to hide my snickering. It seems rude to giggle at a funeral, even if it is for someone no one really likes. One thing you should know about my *late* grandmother is that she's not as dead as everyone thinks. Her ghost happily haunts the three-story Bell, Book & Candle Bookshop she left me in her will, and she also filled an enormous closet with a nearly limitless supply of couture clothing in preparation for her afterlife meeting with me.

The advance invitation to Liliané's exclusive 1920s-themed wake, aboard a riverboat casino, served as the perfect fuel for Grams' insatiable fashion fetish. We have a notorious flapper in our family tree, and my grandmother insisted that we re-create the vintage dress that's on display in my apartment.

"You're right. There's no escaping the noose."

Jacob chuckles. "Let's get out of here. I think we've fulfilled our civic duty."

No need to tell me twice.

After wolfing down my breakfast at Myrtle's Diner, named after Grams and run by her first husband, I return to Bell, Book & Candle to perform wardrobe penance for a ghost.

Having learned the important lesson that patience prevents rumors about crazy ladies who talk to ghosts, I calmly walk through the stacks on the first floor of my bookshop without shouting for my grandmother. I unhook the "No Admittance" chain at the bottom of the wrought-iron circular staircase that leads to my Rare Books Loft, and before the sign even clangs against the railing—

"You better hook that up behind you, Your Highness."

And that would be the un-melodious tones of my one and only employee, Twiggy. Who doesn't actually let me pay her but instead works purely for what she calls "the entertainment." As near as I've been able to tell, during the few months of our arrangement, her amusement comes solely at my expense.

Regardless, I hook the chain behind me and proceed to the loft. Neat rows of oak tables span the mezzanine. Each one has a vintage brass lamp with a green-glass shade. The arms of the balcony stretch around in equal distance, encircling the volumes for sale on the first floor. This building once housed a historic brewery, and Grams kept this cool platform that surrounded the huge brew tanks. The smell of hops and barley is long gone—replaced by the exotic must of rare tomes spilling forth their arcane knowledge.

Currently, this special loft area is for serious research, strictly by appointment. Twiggy handles all of it, and I only get involved if something goes missing. As I reach up to pull down the candle sconce on the wall, which serves as the Scooby-Doo-style handle that opens the sliding bookcase door to my secret apartment, I smile, remembering how Silas and I recovered one such missing volume—*Saducismus Triumphatus*. But that's a whole different story.

The door slides open, and before I can set one foot in the apartment, a frantic apparition hurtles toward me.

"Where have you been? The viewing should've been over an hour ago! I can't find a girdle and I'm certain they've made your dress too small! You'd think my carefully written letters, sketches, and instructions would've been clear! Good help is so hard to find."

Welcome to my world. This is Myrtle Isadora, ghost in residence and grandmother to one Mitzy Moon. I love her to death and beyond, quite literally. And she claims to love me in return, but most days it seems her affection manifests itself best in my *Sex and the City* meets *Confessions of a Shopaholic* closet.

"Look here, young lady, I'll have you know I spent a fortune stocking that closet with clothes, in spite of your father's proclamation that no one in the family should have any contact with you, because, and I quote, 'she's better off without a convict for a father.'"

Bursting into laughter so boisterous that tears leak from the corners of my eyes, I have to lean over and put a hand on my thigh to catch my breath. I can't remember her ever doing an impression of my father before, but I'm definitely hoping there'll be an encore.

She frowns indignantly. "I wasn't trying to be funny."

"All right, that's two." I hold up two fingers and shake my head in warning.

She crosses her bejeweled limbs over her

Marchesa silk-and-tulle burial gown and frowns. "Two what?"

"Two violations of the no-thought-dropping policy. I get that your whole other dimension is made up of a bunch of swirling energy and you can't keep straight if it's my thoughts or your thoughts, but we have a deal." I point meaningfully to my lips. "If these aren't moving, you're not allowed to comment. Now get out of my head and show me this dress you've been working on for two weeks." For a moment her ghostly eyes flare with mischief, but before I can utter a warning, she swirls away toward the closet.

When I walk into the space, which is larger than my former apartment in Sedona, I'm slightly disoriented and can't quite figure out what she's been up to. However, as my eyes drift over the neat racks and shelves, I'm starting to understand the method to her madness.

"Divine, right? I moved all the summer dresses here, all the business suits over here, all the fancy gowns down there—"

"Isadora! What did I just say? If you promise to stay out of my thoughts, I will admit I like the reorganization."

She spins around and her energy glows with happiness. "I knew you'd love it. Now get out of whatever that department store nonsense is, and let's see if we can work with this wardrobe."

Never one to purposefully draw a ghost's anger, I do as I'm told.

I have to put on special 1920s undergarments, some kind of silk slip operation, and finally an immaculately beaded, *Great Gatsby* eat-your-heart-out, flapper dress. Wiggling my hips to help the dress fall into place, I grin as the beaded fringe swings to its own beat below my knees.

Tears spring to Ghost-ma's eyes. "You look like the bee's knees!"

"Oh, brother. One of these days, Grams, I'm going to put Silas's skills to the test and we'll find a way to send a handkerchief into the afterlife."

The ensuing laughter brings additional tears to her eyes. "Enough of this emotional nonsense. Try on the shoes and the fascinator. I need to see the whole look."

I'm pleased that the beautiful red-satin T-strap shoes sport a reasonable two-and-a-half-inch heel. She frequently forces me into teetering stilt shoes that do nothing to diminish my natural clumsiness.

"You're not—"

I stare daggers.

She claps both of her ring-ensconced hands over her mouth and winks.

Shaking my head, I admonish her. "Nothing like a ghost with an addiction to lying."

"Addiction is nothing to joke about, dear. You know my struggle with alcoholism ruined more than one of my marriages."

"Yes, Grams. I wasn't making fun. One day at a time and all that. My apologies."

She swirls around the closet in a bit of a huff, while I fiddle with my diamond-encrusted head-band and the large feathery apparatus hanging off the side.

"Here, let me."

Her ability to pick up and influence objects in the corporeal world is really coming along. When she grabs the headband to make adjustments, it feels almost as if she were alive.

Now we're both crying.

"Thank you, Grams."

"Absolutely any time, my darling granddaugh-ter. But you have to stop making a mess of me. We've got to get your unruly hair into finger waves. They take forever to set."

I step back and kick out one hip. "Do I even want to know what finger waves are?"

She shrugs her designer-gown-clad shoulders and whispers, "It's probably best if you don't."

CHAPTER 2

DREADING THE UNKNOWN, I peel off my dress and hang it up to avoid any phantom retribution, toss my slip on the padded mahogany bench in the center of the closet, and carefully slip off my beautiful ruby slippers.

"Follow me, Mizithra." My ghostly hairstylist blasts through the wall into the bathroom, while I walk around through the doorway like a civilized human.

After what seems like hours of having my head smacked with a hairbrush, while endless amounts of goop are combed through my snow-white locks, I look like a character from *Star Trek: The Next Generation*. I have large metal clips all over my head and I feel like I might be able to pick up extra radio signals even if I didn't have psychic powers.

Slouching in defeat, I ask, "How long?"

Grams sinks down to eye level and arches one perfectly drawn brow. "As long as it takes."

Exhaling dramatically, I pick up my phone. "Fine. I'll be out on the fire escape."

I recently discovered that there's a fire escape out of the back of my second-floor apartment. I've got massive 6 x 6 windows with a gorgeous view of the harbor, immaculate tin-plated ceilings, secret bookcase doors, dream closets, an old-fashioned telephone privacy booth, and now a fire escape.

I climb out the window and text Erick. "Didn't see you at the viewing. Coming to the memorial?"

No reply.

All right. He is a local county sheriff who is, I'm sure, very busy with other people's problems. But I'm kind of his girlfriend now, and I would think my texts would rank very high on his list of daily priorities.

No reply.

I'm not going to be one of those girls . . . I'll watch some videos while I calmly wait.

No reply.

No big deal. I have to sit out here anyway. My hair is certainly not dry. Maybe I'll scroll through some social media and ignore the beads of sweat forming along my hairline.

No reply.

All right. You got me. My breathing is rapid and my heart is having a little infarction. I'm not this calm or this patient. I'm calling. "Yes, hello. May I speak to Sheriff Harper?"

My call is not put through.

"Oh. Yes, it's Mitzy. No, it's not urgent. No, I haven't been kidnapped."

I hang up the phone and I'm half tempted to throw it off the balcony like every scene in every rom-com I've ever watched. The film-school dropout in me is desperate to make that happen, but the recently living below the poverty line me can't see the wisdom in destroying a perfectly good phone.

There's really no reason for me to be upset. According to Furious Monkeys, the nickname I've given the front desk deputy due to her addiction to said game, Erick is on a call. And because she's fairly familiar with my amateur sleuthing, she happened to mention that the call was to the Barnes estate. So, not only am I interested in talking to my sort of boyfriend, Erick Harper, but now I also want to know what the heck is going on out at the manse.

Using the dorky abbreviation for mansion that my father and I used to jokingly bandy about gives me a moment of nostalgia for the old Duncan holdings. I only visited a couple of times, but what a spread!

My practical father sold the estate after my grandpa Cal passed away. He said he didn't need such a big place and that the profits would go a long way to supporting the Duncan Restorative Justice Foundation, an organization my ex-con father generously founded to help defend wrongfully accused prisoners and find good-paying jobs for former criminals. He's trying to do his part to reduce the rate of recidivism.

He's such a great guy. Sure, I wish he had been around when my mother died. Maybe he could've prevented my mostly horrible experiences in foster care, but everything happens for a reason. All of the decisions in my life brought me to this point. Do I have regrets? Yes. Does it make me appreciate what I have now even more? Abso-freaking-lutely!

Hooray, my stupid hair feels crispy. I suppose that's the same as dry?

Climbing back through the window, I call Grams. "Hey! Come and check this weird hairdo. Can we take these cyborg pins off my head?"

Grams blasts through the walls, causing my heart to skip a beat, but, as usual, she has no concern for my earthly fears.

"I seem to remember we agreed on the slow, sparkly re-entry. What happened to that idea?" She completely ignores me.

"Let me see." She carefully fiddles with the clips and touches my crunchy hair.

"What's the verdict?"

"It feels dry, but we're going to leave those clips in for another hour just to be safe."

"You can't be serious."

She places a bejeweled fist on her hip. "Serious as an angry spirit."

I know the ominous words are supposed to scare me, but when they're coming from the loving face of a woman who died in her sixties but selected the youthful ghost age of thirty-five, it feels more like a comedy scene from Gene Wilder's *Young Frankenstein.*

I bow like a marionette on strings. "I am yours to command, Great Ghost-ma."

"Oh Mitzy, you're a hoot."

Shortly after taking possession of the bookstore, I discovered that Ghost-ma's lawyer, Silas Willoughby, a dangerously skilled alchemist, had devised a way to tether her spirit to the bookshop rather than let her cross over.

It definitely took some getting used to, living with a ghost, and there were a few unfortunate pants accidents. But now that Ghost-ma and I have some ground rules, we're getting along fine—when she bothers to follow the rules. Apart from a few missteps, I'm learning to co-exist with her and her fiendish feline.

After my mother's untimely death, I entered the foster system at the age of eleven and never had a pet of my own. Sure, I got to watch my foster siblings care for various animals over the years, but strictly as an outsider. So, inheriting a fairly dangerous, semi-wild tan caracal with black tufts on his ears, scars over his left eye, and an addiction to sugary children's cereal is almost more of an adjustment than living with a ghost.

But, in the end, I have to say Ghost-ma wins the award for most difficult. Let's take tonight's event for example. The recently deceased Liliané Barnes is the only woman in town who rivals my grandmother in both wealth and ex-husbands. So when we received the extravagant hand-delivered invitation to her memorial service, Myrtle Isadora Johnson Linder Duncan Willamet Rogers insisted I attend.

Of course, her demands included my father's participation. Regardless of his tireless work at the Duncan Restorative Justice Foundation, she implored him to procure the appropriate costume and escort me to the event.

Cut to—

. . .

"Mitzy, are you in there?" My dad gently taps my knee as he eases his vehicle to a stop.

The film-school dropout in me is hesitant to tear my gaze away from the three decks of glittering lights floating on the great lake. "Hey, sorry. I guess I drifted off. Are you ready for this?"

Jacob chuckles. "I don't think your grandmother much cares whether or not we're ready. She expects a full report. If there are any socialites in attendance that weren't at her memorial service, I shudder to think . . ."

"You're not wrong."

My father parks his 1955 Ford F100, pleads with me to remain seated, and circles around to help me out of the truck.

Despite my fierce independent woman *insides*, my elaborate flapper getup needs all the assistance it can get. Trust me when I tell you, Grams went all out! I had to flee my own apartment to stop the ceaseless addition of accoutrements.

I'll start at the top and work my way down. I have a diamond-encrusted headband displaying a large ruby pendant festooned with red and black ostrich feathers. Draped over my left shoulder is a beautiful, black faux-mink stole. Around my neck hangs an enormous strand of pearls knotted in front so they don't slip off my shoulders, and underneath it all—an amazing hand-beaded, red-fringed flapper dress. I look like an Anita Page publicity photo!

The lines of the dress magically disguise my slightly bottom-heavy build. There are two or three layers involved. I can't even keep track. One of the under-layers is creamy white silk, and the outer layer is a filmy sheath embellished with hundreds and hundreds of Swarovski crystals. The red-and-silver theme catches the lights of the casino boat, and I sparkle like a Vegas marquee. My feet are encased in vintage 1920s red-satin T-straps.

My father opted to steer clear of the traditional pinstripe gangster suit, in an effort to avoid any comparison to his youthful indiscretions. I mean, he was involved in an armed robbery and served time in the state penitentiary, so he chose a classy, above-reproach 1920s tuxedo.

Not to brag, but we make a striking pair. Our matching snow-white hair, his slicked back under a top hat and mine in dramatic finger waves, turns a number of heads as we approach the gangplank. A young man in costume at the bottom checks the guest list and announces us as we board. Any heads that weren't already turned certainly whip-pan in our direction as our names echo over the loud-speaker.

I may not have been able to afford to finish film school, but I learned enough to know that this is definitely what we call in the business "making an entrance."

Thankfully, my father walks directly to the bar.

"I will absolutely have a glass of champagne, Dad."

He grins. "And I'll have whatever the signature cocktail is. I'm not sure how much longer I can take all these eyes turned in our direction."

And before we can suffer any additional discomfort, the next guest is announced and all eyes are redirected toward the gangplank.

Now that we're no longer the center of attention, I take a minute to scan the crowd. A few faces are familiar from this morning's viewing, but there are at least three times more people in attendance at this celebration of life. Apparently, we somehow qualified as part of her private viewing inner circle, even though, to the best of my knowledge, she and my grandmother seemed more like arch-rivals than friends.

I down my coupe of champagne and tap the bar for another while my father elegantly sips his "Bee's Knees."

The flirtatious boy-toy-turned-widower that Liliané collected on her *Eat, Pray, Love* tour of Greece approaches the microphone—as smoldering as ever.

I can't wait to hear if this announcement will

ring as hollow as his endless words of sorrow from this morning.

"Welcome, friends. Liliané wanted all of us to celebrate her life. Please eat, drink, and gamble. She will certainly be looking down on us from heaven. Let's not disappoint my beautiful angel." His full red lips pucker and he blows a kiss heavenward, before signaling the band. A lively, upbeat, jazzy version of the Charleston song bursts to life.

Leaning toward my dad, I whisper, "Is it just me, or does he sound as fake as a three-dollar bill?"

My father chokes a little on his cocktail. "I was thinking the same thing." He leans closer and lowers his voice. "Are you getting any, you know, messages?"

My psychic gifts have been evolving ever since I arrived in this remote northern community. It all started the day I put on my grandmother's 1970s mood ring and had a gripping clairsentient experience. Now I regularly receive visions, auditory messages, feelings, and inexplicable knowings. But at this moment, the mood ring on my left hand is offering no information about the superficial widower. "The one thing I can say, is that I think a brooch was missing from Liliané's lapel and something felt weird about the body this morning. Well, that was two things. But I can't explain it, her body felt hollow."

To Jacob's credit he makes no mockery of my strange revelation. "Well, it was a corpse. They are kind of hollow by definition, right?"

I nod. "Yeah, but in my experience there's a heaviness to the finality. Something felt off about her—corpse. Is that weird?"

He smiles down at me and shrugs his broad shoulders. "You get psychic messages from some dimension I don't even understand. I had to move weird to the back burner when you came into my life."

I roll my eyes and snicker. "Rude, but accurate."

Jacob nudges me with his elbow, and I gaze up at him questioningly. "What?"

He nods toward the stage. "I think you're gonna want to see this."

As my eyes struggle to take in the scene, a mixture of fear and anger swirls in my belly.

A commanding Native American woman in an exquisite white flapper dress, white ostrich feather boa, and pearl tiara, takes center stage. She's flanked by two intimidatingly large Native American bodyguards, clad in, all too appropriate, mobster pinstripes.

I grip my father's arm and hiss, "Shouldn't she be in jail?"

His head swivels back and forth in disdain, but

his eyes never leave the stage. "Shhh, we'll talk about that later."

My moody mood ring offers no clue to explain the apparent freedom of the woman who set my dad up to take the fall for her illegal deeds.

The powerful woman on the dais compels the guests' attention, even before she speaks. All eyes turn to take in the dramatic entrance.

She grips the microphone with one white-gloved hand and begins her speech. "Ladies and gentlemen, Leticia Whitecloud welcomes you to the Hawk Island Floating Casino."

A smattering of applause drifts through the crowd as the audience exchanges confused glances.

Trust me, I know exactly how they feel. I wish I could jump up on stage and let them all know that the woman in front of them *is* Leticia Whitecloud. That, in fact, Leticia Whitecloud talks about herself in the third person, and no matter how long they wait for what they believe will be the entrance of the aforementioned Leticia Whitecloud, she's already on stage.

"Please enjoy the hors d'oeuvres and the cash bar. As per Liliané Barnes' request, champagne will be complimentary all evening. Leticia Whitecloud would like you to know that all gambling is legitimate. If you lose you lose for real, if you win . . ."

She exchanges an unreadable glance with her two goons. "Then, congratulations."

The audience whispers in earnest, and I overhear the couple next to me. "Where's this Leticia Whitecloud?" the elderly man asks as he taps his hearing aid.

The woman replies, "No idea, dear. Did she say this is real gambling? I thought it was for some charity or something."

The man shrugs. "Well, I'm not gambling with real money."

The woman, whom I take to be his wife, crosses her arms severely. "That's for sure."

Before I have a chance to discuss the inappropriateness of profiting off someone's death, my dad grabs my arm and tugs me down a narrow passageway between the brilliantly lit railing and the roulette room.

"What's going on?"

"She saw me."

"Good. Let's go have it out with her."

"I don't think that's a good idea. In fact, I think we should try to avoid her for the rest of the evening."

"Look, Dad, she's the one who should've been in jail for life. How do you explain her walking free a few months later?"

Before my father can answer, a familiar mo-
notone voice behind me says, "Money."

I spin on my two-inch satin heels, and I'm face-
to-face with Leticia Whitecloud.

For some reason, I always get the nervous grins
around this woman. There she stands in all white,
like an angel, and here I am in all red, like a devil.
When, in fact, the roles are quite reversed.

"Leticia Whitecloud does not see the humor in
this meeting, Ms. Moon."

The bodyguard named Jimmy, if I remember
correctly, is approaching from behind my father.

My extra senses pick up on a surge of anger and
overprotectiveness from my father as he widens his
stance.

"Don't do anything stupid, all right, Dad?"

"You should listen to your wise daughter, Jacob
Duncan."

Ignoring her attempt to incite a reaction from
my father, I go on the offensive. "So you bribed your
way out of jail, Ms. Whitecloud?"

"Leticia Whitecloud is a law-abiding sovereign
citizen. My attorney simply made that clear to the
court."

Jimmy puts a hand on my father's shoulder.

Before I can utter a warning, my dad grips his
wrist, fully flips the guy through the air, over his
shoulder, and onto his back. And as Jimmy hits the

deck, my father yanks the gun out of Jimmy's shoulder holster, pulls me toward him, and aims the pistol at Leticia.

"Stay down, Jimmy." The harsh edge in my father's voice makes the hairs on the back of my neck stand on end.

"Leticia Whitecloud doesn't think felons are meant to have guns, Duncan."

I reach a shaky hand toward my father's wrist. "Dad, please give me the gun."

Fear and frustration roll off him in waves. He doesn't hand me the gun, but he doesn't resist as I carefully slip it out of his grasp.

However, I don't return the weapon to the *muscle*. Instead, I address Leticia with the added encouragement of the gun aimed at her midsection. "Do you mind telling me how you managed to get involved in this memorial service?"

Jimmy is clearly not as intimidated by me as he was by my father, and he slowly gets to his feet, placing his body directly in the line of fire.

The narrow passageway doesn't allow me to get a better angle, so I calmly keep the weapon trained on the nearest target.

Leticia's voice replies from behind the broad shoulders of her protector. "We are acquainted with the deceased's husband."

The three of them chuckle briefly.

"It looks like we're all going to be on this boat together for the next two hours, Ms. Whitecloud. I'm going to hang on to this gun. You and your—employees—steer clear of me and my dad, and we'll do the same. I'm sure it wouldn't take long for Sheriff Harper to intercept your little floating tax shelter. Do we understand one another?"

Jimmy looks toward my father, and, if I didn't know better, they seem to be exchanging some silent agreement. But before I have time to analyze that, Leticia replies, "You may appear to be the deer, but you are the wolf. Leticia Whitecloud respects this."

I manage to do my best impression of a Robert De Niro head nod and slip the gun into my handbag.

Jimmy turns and escorts his boss below decks.

My dad immediately reaches for my handbag.

"Hey, have you taken to purse snatching now?"

My inappropriate dark humor does the trick. My father chuckles softly. "Actually, I want to make sure you have the safety on that thing, Don Corleone."

"Copy that."

Once he's confirmed that the safety is on, he snaps my handbag closed and walks toward the bar.

I hesitantly grab his sleeve, eager to avoid a fate similar to Jimmy's. "Um, Dad, you want to tell me what's going on between you and Whitecloud's goon?"

He turns. "What do you— Never mind. I should know better than to try to sneak anything past you and all your special senses."

I cross my arms, tilt my head, and wait for an answer to my question.

"This stays between us. Just us, understood?"

Despite my rebellious nature, there's something in my father's tone that compels agreement. "I promise. Just between us."

"When I was locked up in Clearwater, Jimmy's son got done for a dime. Based on what we know about Leticia, it's hard to say if the kid was guilty, or if he was another pawn in her great game of ruining lives."

I nod. "So you're saying Jimmy's not loyal to her?"

My father shakes his head fervently. "I'm not saying that at all. Jimmy will go to the grave protecting her. But one of the opposing gangs cornered Jimmy's son in the yard. I'm pretty sure they would've killed him if I hadn't stepped in."

My throat tightens, my eyes mist with emotion, and I lift my chin. "Why would you do that? Why would you risk your life for someone you didn't even know?"

He exhales slowly. "Jimmy and I went to school

together. He wasn't always a two-bit criminal. His kid was barely nineteen, had his whole life ahead of him. I guess I couldn't stop myself."

I dab my finger under my eyes to prevent any telltale mascara streaks. "Didn't they just turn on you?"

"Briefly." He smirks.

I step back and appraise my father's massive shoulders, barrel chest, and thick arms. "Did you put the hurt on 'em?"

The serious tone of our conversation evaporates and he laughs with relief. "You could say that."

"So, in spite of his loyalty to Leticia, Jimmy's got mad respect for you."

Jacob shakes his head in amusement. "Nobody cuts to the heart of things like you, Mitzy."

"Speaking of . . . How do you want to do this? I think it's probably best if you gamble and I snoop?"

My father wipes a hand across his weary brow. "I'll assume there's no point in arguing?"

"Sounds good, Ace. I hope you get some hot dice."

I can see my father's shoulders quake with laughter as he heads toward the craps table.

Now I need to find this red-hot widower—easy girl—and see how it is that he's *acquainted* with Leticia Whitecloud.

CHAPTER 3

TAKING THE NARROW STAIRS down to the middle deck, I'm met with the odor of stale cigarette smoke and the desperate and grating laughter of a woman. When I enter the smoking lounge adjacent to the poker tables, the small, dark, and handsome widower is the cause of her performance.

According to Grams, the marriage was barely three years old. Liliané's eighth husband died of a heart attack during a bungee jumping excursion in New Zealand. Rumor has it she was so devastated, she had to mourn her way around the globe.

When she walked into a taverna on Mykonos and saw Vassili tending bar, it was love at first sight.

Grams assures me that the love was one-sided until Vassili caught sight of Liliané's bank balance. When she returned to Pin Cherry with a husband thirty-plus years her junior, the backlash was scandalous!

He definitely looks like a gigolo, and the way he's flirting with this slightly older woman indicates his brief mourning period has ended and he's ready to jump into yet another deeply meaningful financial relationship.

I order champagne, take a seat at the bar, and pretend to gaze longingly toward the twinkling lights of Pin Cherry Harbor. Meanwhile, all my senses, the regular ones and the extras, are trained on Mr. Vassili Barnes. Yes, that's right, he took her last name.

"The deep purple in that amethyst torque brings out the hidden violet flecks in your eyes."

"Please don't use my sister's name."

Uh oh, scandal—part two. I thought that chick looked familiar. The woman he's flirting with is Iris, the older, married daughter of the deceased. I didn't recognize her at first with the masses of ringlets and a sparkly gown softening her angular features. Not to mention the exposed sinewy muscles on her arms that were previously hidden by her tailored black mourning suit.

Vassili reaches gentle fingers toward her rouged cheek.

But the reflection I'm watching in the window

steps back and firmly pushes his eager hand away with her gloved one. "Not here."

"Then you had better leave, my love. I'm unable to restrain myself in your presence."

My clairsentience picks up on her mixture of guilt and longing. The yuck factor, of the two of them being involved in an affair behind her mother's back, is pretty huge.

She manages to tear herself away and scurry toward the stairs.

He disappears through a door behind the bar, and I'm unable to stop myself from following.

The narrow door leads into a small, mid-ship supply room with a hatch, and a ladder stretching down to the deck below. I step toward the opening and the sound of his retreating footsteps signals, hopefully, all clear.

Managing slick metal ladder rungs in a bedazzled flapper dress and heels is certainly not as easy as they make it look in the movies. By the time I reach the bottom, my headband is slipping on my sweaty brow and the silk under-layers of my getup are sticking to my lower back, and other places.

As I struggle to adjust my slip, a server walks in to retrieve a stack of napkins. "Hey, you're not supposed to be back here."

Here goes nothing.

Engage bimbo voice. "Right? I'll be out of your

hair in a minute. This humidity . . . and my slip." I hike my dress up to reveal my garter stockings and bend over to make the most out of my cleavage as I tug on the silk lining.

The young man's cheeks flush and he hurries out, mumbling over his shoulder. "Sure, whatever. Take your time."

I shimmy my shoulders and wish Grams were here to share in my success. "Still got it."

Unfortunately, the delay causes me to temporarily lose track of my quarry. I peek out of the door leading toward the stern, but there's no sign of our lech-in-mourning.

Back through the storage area and out the other side leads into a private poker game.

There's no sign of Vassili, but my mood ring finally sparks to life. I glance down in time to make out the image of a polished wooden door.

Smiling nervously at the players, I hustle across the room, exit through the other door, and take the stairs below decks.

The bow of the boat houses a limited number of suites. I step quietly along the passageway and, as I near the polished wooden door, familiar from my vision, I hear the unmistakable sound of a bereaved husband seeking solace in the arms of another woman.

Based on my earlier eavesdropping, I feel certain I've stumbled upon Vassili and Iris. I carefully twist the handle to the room across the hall from their tryst, and the door opens easily.

Stepping inside what luckily turns out to be an empty cabin, I close the door to a narrow slit and wait to confirm my suspicions.

Disappointingly, for Iris, Vassili exits their room less than five minutes later. He heads back up top, and I wait for Iris to clear out before I leave my hiding place. I'd very much like to avoid being caught.

Imagine my surprise when a youthful cocktail waitress emerges, still tucking in her shirt, oblivious to her smeared lipstick.

She hustles off in the opposite direction from her rendezvous partner.

As soon as she's out of sight, I follow. No point in walking through that private poker game twice.

I lose her on the top deck and double back to see if I can pick up Vassili's trail.

As I approach the stern, the raised voices of two men arguing send me skulking into the shadows to eavesdrop.

"I don't care what my mother's supposed will said, you cheap piece of Euro-trash. You're not getting her money."

"No. No. We are family, Roman. There's no need for you to be upset about the love I shared with your mother. I will make sure you and your sisters are well cared for."

A nauseous swirl surges toward my esophagus. If Roman had any idea how Vassili was taking care of Iris, he'd probably push him overboard right now.

Creeping stealthily toward the commotion, I clasp my hand over my mouth and hope my prediction isn't about to come true.

Roman has a handful of Vassili's shirt and he's pushing him backward over the railing.

The lover-not-a-fighter is struggling, but he's smaller than the Prince Harry doppelganger and not driven by vindictive rage.

Before I can shout out a warning, Leticia and her goons walk onto the deck.

"Back away from him." Her voice is low and even. The naturally flat affect carries no hint of concern. She speaks from a place of absolute belief in her instructions being unquestionably followed.

Jimmy closes the distance in two strides and grabs Roman by the scruff of the neck. He tosses him toward his partner. "Arnie, take the kid below deck till he cools down."

Vassili grips the railing with one hand and straightens out his shirt with the other. "Thank you. I'm not sure what has so upset him."

"Leticia Whitecloud does not care about your family squabbles. You promised us that the take from this pathetic memorial service would cover your debts. So far, the shortfall is enormous."

"I— I have all the money now," he stutters. "Just be patient until the accounts are transferred over. I can easily pay you in a couple of weeks."

Jimmy's thick hand grips Vassili around the throat.

Leticia steps forward.

"Time's up."

The bodyguard lifts Vassili off the ground and the poor man's feet kick helplessly.

I can't watch another minute of this. "Hey, Vassili, I've been looking for you." I stride across the deck as though I haven't seen or heard a thing. "I need someone to show me how to play craps."

Jimmy lowers our host back to the deck, and as soon as his feet touch the wooden surface, Vassili hurries to me.

Stepping toward the criminal element, I adopt a light, airy tone. "Oh, hello again, Ms. Whitecloud. I hope you're enjoying the beautiful evening on the water."

The mobster queen makes no verbal reply, but I'm fortunate to have a vast array of other senses. And they are all screaming to get below deck.

I hook my arm through Vassili's elbow and tug him toward the bow. "So you and Liliané met in Greece?"

As we reach the narrow stairway to the middle deck, the tear-stained face of Iris appears below us. "Is it true?"

There is a distinct "cheating cheater" vibe in the air, and it's time for me to make myself scarce. "Thanks for showing me to the stairs. I have to be getting back to my father." I unhook my arm from Vassili's elbow and slip past Iris.

She doesn't even wait until I'm out of sight. "Is it true, Vassili? I heard some waitress talking about hooking up with you? She was telling one of the other help that you promised to take her to Mykonos. Is it true?"

Time to find another route to the main deck and ask my father if he has any idea how to get us off this boat before the scheduled return to the docks.

Apparently, it's way easier to follow someone blindly around the convoluted passageways on a vessel than it is to navigate one's own path.

After three wrong turns and a random toss at the craps table, I give up and grab a coupe of champagne. It feels too Sedona woo-woo to say, but when you stop seeking and release the outcome—

I spy my father's slicked-back swath of bone-white hair nodding politely as two dowagers entertain him with their tales.

Casually bobbing my head back and forth, in what I hope is a subtle attempt to get his attention, I wait to be noticed. But before I find success, a blood-curdling scream rips through the night.

All heads turn toward the disruption, and my father knifes through the crowd to scoop a protective arm around my shoulders.

The ring on my left hand turns to ice and I glance down in time to see a rope.

The stomach-churning chill twisting around my spine can't possibly mean anything good.

CHAPTER 4

MY FINGERS DIAL the number before my brain has time to realize what's happening.

"Erick? You better get to the marina."

His first question is to confirm that I'm all right, which is adorable and deserves acknowledgment, but my gratitude will have to wait. Instead, I quickly fill him in on the events aboard the *Jewel of the Harbor*. And, sorry to have to say this, but those events include a body dangling from a rope secured to the railing of the top deck.

My father, Jimmy, and Arnie have secured a perimeter on both the middle and top decks.

While the captain steers the boat back toward its mooring, the guests dash about, frantically gazing at everyone with heightened suspicion.

I kick my extrasensory perceptions into overdrive and hunt for clues.

Leticia Whitecloud is nowhere to be found. At this point, I'm not sure if that makes her guilty or innocent, but it's worth noting.

Roman Barnes has bellied up to the bar and, in the short time since the scream alerted us all to the unfortunate incident, he's thrown back at least two whiskeys and tossed a crumpled cigarette pack on the deck.

For some inexplicable reason the band is still playing a jazzy Charleston, and for a moment I feel as though I'm aboard the *Titanic*, and we're all supposed to pretend that everything's all right as we slowly drown.

Slipping down the ladder I discovered earlier, I'm surprised to find the private poker game still in session. However, this time when I pass through the room, one of the players looks up.

"What's all the commotion up top?"

"I can't say for certain it's murder, but Vassili Barnes is dead."

Murmurs circle around the poker table and a small, nervous man suggests they call it a night.

The dealer stops shuffling and waits for consensus.

The man who posed the original question about the commotion seems to hold sway over the rest of the players. "Not on your life, Dickens. It's not our fault if you don't know when to quit. We finish this hand, and then you pay up."

My clairsentience picks up on a visceral wave of fear from the man called Dickens. I can safely assume he's unable to cover his bet. Not my concern.

Sneaking down the back stairs, I check the suites below deck. All empty—this time.

As I pass through a stretch of the passageway with no hatches, I get a strange tingling on my ring finger. I look down and simply see polished wood paneling. But I have more than the average passenger's experience with secret doorways, and something about the tingling and the image stirs my curiosity.

I run my hand over the paneling near the top of the wall and feel an indentation hidden in the shadow. Hesitantly slipping my finger in, I press. A section of the paneling pops open, and I'm not entirely surprised to be gazing into the somewhat shocked face of Leticia Whitecloud.

Pushing the door fully open, I smile. "Ms. Whitecloud, I'm sure you'll want to come above deck to speak to the sheriff about the murder that so recently occurred on your gambling boat." Without waiting for a reply, I turn and rush down the passageway before she can pull out the gun she most certainly has in her pearl evening bag.

Racing up the stairs near the bow, I come face-to-face with Iris and her husband. She's shaking her head in violent disagreement, and he's mumbling in a very menacing tone.

They both fall absolutely still and silent when they see me. Maybe she needs some kind of bailout from this threatening exchange. I'm nothing if not helpful—and curious—but mostly helpful.

"I'm sorry, aren't you Iris? Roman was looking for you. He's at the bar on the main deck. He seems very upset."

After dispensing the lie, I sink into my psychic gifts. Iris seems to seal herself off in a prison of ice, while her husband's anger instantly shifts to protectiveness.

He grips her firmly by the arm and tugs her back up the stairway. "Come along, Iris. Let's go to deal with your insufferable baby brother."

Jeezy creezy. Not all families are created equal, that's for sure.

I hurry up the steps after them, but my stomach swirls with a flash of nausea as the boat slows and spins awkwardly in the water. We must be nearing the docks in the marina, and I definitely want to get my hands on Erick before anyone else does.

Racing to the port side as we slowly motor toward the dock, I search the shore and find the sheriff and four of his deputies waiting on the gangplank.

As soon as the boat comes in range, two dockworkers, probably conscripted by Erick, tie off the boat. Two deputies man the gangplank, ensuring that no one exits without an interview, while Erick, flanked by Deputy Paulsen and Furious Monkeys/Deputy Baird, boards the ship with the confidence and bluster of an old-fashioned pirate raid.

While I make a beeline for Erick, he nods in my direction and sends Paulsen toward the body.

By the time I reach the sheriff, Deputy Baird has commandeered the microphone and is directing the passengers to "form a queue on the main deck . . ." The rest of her speech is lost as I let Erick slip a protective arm around my waist.

"How do you get yourself into these things, Moon?"

"Let me remind you, I'm a guest, Sheriff Harper, not a suspect."

He shakes his head. "No, you're not a suspect—this time. But that doesn't mean you're not under suspicion."

"Before you waltz too far down that road, Sheriff, I thought you might like to know that the victim argued with several people over the course of the evening, and nearly all the female attendees are wearing gloves. Oh, also, it might interest you that Leticia Whitecloud, Jimmy, and Arnie are running this operation."

Erick raises his eyebrows and nods thoughtfully. "I was made aware of her involvement by the Tribal Council. I'm sure there was some bribery and possibly even some blackmail involved. But I'm curious to know your source?"

I open my mouth to answer—

"Welcome aboard, Sheriff Harper. Let Leticia Whitecloud know if there is anything the boys can do for you."

Erick takes in the vision in white that is Leticia Whitecloud and tilts his head my way.

Smiling, I whisper, "Asked and answered, your honor."

He slips past me to continue his investigation, and I suddenly feel the burning need to find the demure Violet Barnes. My search below deck was fairly thorough, but I have yet to make it topside. I casually wander toward the staircase at the bow of the vessel and climb to the uppermost deck.

There, leaning over the railing, weeping and tossing bits of torn paper into the lake, is Violet.

Approaching slowly, I offer my condolences. "Excuse me, it's Violet isn't it? I'm so sorry about this second tragedy."

She turns and the harbor lights reveal streaked

mascara and swollen eyes. "I actually loved my mother, you know. Iris doesn't speak for all of us. Vassili made my mom happy."

I close the distance and gently pat her shoulder. "I'm glad to know your mother was happy at the end. So many of us never have that chance."

"I knew something terrible was going to happen —after that huge fight at the estate. I don't understand why she left everything to Vassili in the will? She could've tossed a few thousand dollars to Iris and Roman. That's all they cared about. Money! When they found out she left everything to *him*, they lost it. You know?"

I'm pretty sure I've cracked the case regarding what "call" Erick was on earlier. And why he was so *un*surprised to hear about the tragedy during tonight's memorial service.

"What about you? Didn't you want anything of your mother's?"

She sniffles loudly. "Maybe a few knickknacks, just memories. Vassili said he would see that we were all taken care of. I don't know what the big deal was."

"You said you were worried something like this would happen. Did someone threaten violence this afternoon?" Fortunately, the bereaved younger sister is too emotional to be suspicious.

"Not exactly. Roman said he'd find a way to invalidate the will, and Iris said she'd never let Vassili walk away with everything, but no one threatened to kill him."

At the mention of Vassili's murder, my mood ring turns icy, and I glance down to see an encore presentation of the rope.

"Violet, was it you that screamed—before, I mean?"

Her innocence vanishes in a heartbeat, and the bitter stain that taints her sister's beauty bubbles to the surface. "Who did you say you were?"

"I'm Mitzy. My grandmother was a close friend of your mother."

She steps away, and her sorrow turns to distrust. "My mother didn't have any friends. Especially not ones her own age." Violet turns to leave, but trips on her own shoe.

I instinctively reach out to steady her. "Are you okay? Is something wrong with your shoe?"

She yanks her arm from my grasp, adjusts her boa with a gloved hand, and marches toward the stairs with an uneven gait.

There's no point hurrying after her. I've gotten all the information I can from Violet Barnes.

Heading down a deck, toward the gangplank to check in with Erick, I notice the crowd is wadding up around the exit like a herd of sheep at the gate. But these sheep are getting restless and angry.

I force my way through the crowd with some nonsense comments about having important information for the sheriff, but when I arrive and see the two deputies barely keeping the agitated guests on board, I hastily make a new plan.

"Hey, Deputy?"

The thick-necked one with black hair looks up questioningly.

I nod. "Yeah, you'll do. Did you get a copy of the guest list?"

His eyes register more anxiety than his powerful stance would indicate as he shakes his head.

I turn and address the crowd in my "last call" voice. "Has anyone seen the young kid who checked you in and announced your name when you boarded?"

Most shake their head, but, lucky for me, the kid I'm talking about is hidden amongst the crowd and pushes his way forward. "Do you mean me?"

"Depends. You got the guest list?"

He waves his clipboard and nods.

"Make way, folks. Make way. Once he gets us that guest list, we'll have you out of here in fifteen minutes."

The crowd parts like the Red Sea, and a high-school-age boy in an ill-fitting gangster suit rushes forward.

He hands me the clipboard. "Um, so, I'm not on

that list, but I gotta get home. My mom has to work the graveyard shift at the cannery and I gotta babysit my little sister."

"Come with me. And keep your mouth shut."

The scrawny teenager falls in line behind me.

I approach the two deputies. "Deputy— Does your name tag say 'Johnson'? Any relation to Odell?"

He shakes his head. "No relation. I get that a lot, though. Myrtle's Diner is pretty popular and folks say I kinda look like him."

He absolutely looks nothing like Odell Johnson, my grandmother's first husband and my surrogate grandfather, but, like Grams always says, more flies with honey. "Sure, I can see that. I tell you what, I've got something here that's going to make your job real easy and I only need a tiny favor in exchange."

He looks at the angry mob behind me, leans forward and whispers, "You're the one dating the sheriff, right?"

I grin. "Correct."

"Whatever you say goes."

I gotta say, I'm liking this Deputy Johnson more and more by the minute. "Here's a clipboard with the entire guest list. This wonderful young man made a checkmark by each name as they boarded the vessel. Now he's gotta go, immediately—that's the favor—and all you have to do is read off these names and make a little X when they leave. I'll ask them if they have any helpful information or saw anything suspicious. If we work on this together, we should have them out of here in no time. The fact is, everyone was up on the main deck waiting for the door prize to be awarded. Do we have a deal?"

He takes the clipboard, pulls a pen from his pocket and says, "Let's do this."

The young man, whose name I'm sorry to say I didn't ask, runs down the gangplank and sprints toward the bus stop.

Boy, do I remember those days.

The deputy begins calling the roll, and I casually question the guests as they pass by. As predicted, everyone was on the main deck hoping that his or her name would be called for the door prize.

As we wait for a particularly ancient couple to hobble down the gangplank with a walker and a four-footed cane, Deputy Johnson asks, "What was the door prize?"

"Three hundred dollars—in chips—to be used aboard the *Jewel of the Harbor*."

He scoffs. "What a racket."

I tilt my head in agreement. "You're not wrong."

The elderly pair, Erma and Willard, finally reach us. I don't need to ask if they saw anything, because I don't think either of them has seen anything or heard anything in a decade. The Deputy and I exchange knowing glances, and his partner gestures for the couple to disembark.

"Did they say if there was going to be cake?" Erma shouts to her husband as they toddle down the gangway.

He hollers back, "I'm sure there'll be another wake, Erma. Somebody said something about another dead guy."

Deputy Johnson plows through the remainder of the guest list. By the time we reach the inner circle of family, Violet has taken off her shoes and refuses to make eye contact with me.

Not to be rude, but she looks positively horrible. Her skin is a greenish hue, indicating perhaps late onset seasickness? A combination of smeared mascara and eyeliner makes dark circles under her eyes, and her finger waves have waved bye-bye!

"Just the family left, right?" Deputy Johnson asks.

"Right, and the crew. That's Violet there, the middle child. I don't see Roman, but I assume he's still at the bar. And behind Violet is the oldest sister, Iris Barnes-Becker, and her husband whose first name I don't actually know."

Deputy Johnson runs his pen across the page. "Says here it's Tom."

"You better take statements from the family. I

don't think they were waiting to find out who won the door prize, and according to some insider information they pretty much all have motives."

"Thank you, Miss Moon. We'll take it from here. I sure do appreciate you calming the angry masses." He smiles and nods gratefully. "I guess it's true what they say about you."

Pasting on a fake smile, I hope that what they say about me is that I'm a wonderfully kind person, and I'm crossing my fingers that no one is saying anything to this deputy about my psychic powers, or suspicion thereof. "I hope it's all good." A strangled chuckle escapes.

"Pretty much. No one really listens to Paulsen."

This information produces a genuine belly laugh, which I immediately attempt to hide, because it seems kind of rude to laugh at a memorial service turned murder scene. "Pleasure working with you, Deputy Johnson. Good luck with the statements."

He tips his chin, and I hurry up the gangplank to find Erick.

As I approach the back of the boat, raised voices echo off the water.

"I'm not the least bit interested in what kind of immunity you think you have, Whitecloud. The murder was committed on your vessel and we're impounding it until the crime is solved. If you have any helpful information you'd like to share to speed things along, Johnson and Gilbert will be happy to take your statements when you leave the boat."

Leticia steps closer to Erick and lowers her voice to almost a whisper. "Leticia Whitecloud doesn't forget, Sheriff."

She turns and shoves past me. I teeter over the railing, but I'm in no real danger.

Jimmy and Arnie follow close behind, but surprisingly have the courtesy to turn sideways as they pass me rather than dog pile on their boss's rudeness.

Last in line is my father. The strain on his face would be evident even to a daughter without special gifts. But I sense the fear and anxiety underneath his exhaustion. "We should probably get out of here, Dad."

He leans toward me and whispers, "Are you sure you're done snooping?"

"Rude." But his comment does get me thinking. "Actually, can you distract Erick for a few minutes? There's something I need to grab on the upper deck."

He exhales and his shoulders slump. "I wasn't serious."

"Don't ask the question if you don't want to know the answer." I spin around on my ruby slippers and hoof it up to the top deck.

Kneeling near where I found Violet weeping earlier, I collect all the torn pieces of paper that didn't make it into the great lake. Then I circle around to the stern and take a careful panoramic mental picture, for later enhanced psychic replay.

The railing.

The deck.

The rope.

All the tools involved in ending Vassili's life.

CHAPTER 5

"Grams? Grams? Don't you want to hear about
the memorial service?" Normally she can't hear me
when she's up on the third floor of the printing museum working on her memoirs, but something
must've tickled her ghostly senses, because she
rockets through the wall into the bookshop aglow
with anticipation.

"I want to know the names of everyone who
was there. If there was anyone in attendance that
didn't come to my service . . . Well, I'm sure there's
something a ghost of my status could do."

"So you don't want to hear about the murder?"

"Liliané was murdered?"

"Not that I know of, but someone left Vassili
dangling at the end of his rope."

She gasps dramatically. "Oh, how terrible! He was so handsome."

"Wow. I'm pretty sure it's sad when ugly people die too, Grams."

She waves her hand at me dismissively. "Mitzy, that's not what I meant, and you know it."

"Lucky for you, I'm the only one who can hear you. And who am I gonna tell? I don't think there's a long line of people who will believe that I talk to the ghost of my dead grandmother."

"Mitzy!"

"Sorry! Is it life-challenged? I can't remember what we settled on."

"It's fine, dear. God grant me the serenity to accept the things I cannot change. By all normal standards, I am dead. That's the truth."

"Well, the nice thing is the Duncan-Moons don't really live in the world of normal standards. Now, are you going to help me set up this murder wall, or do I have to solve all the mysteries myself?"

As I wander over to the rolling board, Grams zooms through me and sends me into a fit of giggles. Since I've always been able to see her, I've never gotten the ghost-chills when she enters the room or comes near me. There's something wonderful about our connection and I will forever be indebted to the curmudgeonly Silas Willoughby.

"You write out the cards. I'll tack 'em up and tie

the string. The green string, because red gives you the frights."

"Copy that," she replies. Grams' ghostly snicker at her appropriation of my phrase warms my heart.

I roll the corkboard into the middle of the room, careful not to bump into any of the precious Italian plaster walls that Twiggy is so eager to protect, and start calling out the names. "Let's get a card for every member of the Barnes family and, of course, for Vassili. You've been in the same social circles as Liliané. Can you think of any enemies she had?"

Grams floats over and hands me the cards for the three children. "We don't have enough 3 x 5 cards, dear. That woman was cruel, devious, and wealthy. The trifecta in the rich b—"

"Grams! Language."

"Sorry. It's just . . . She was always outbidding me at charity auctions, always trying to make slightly larger donations. She even insisted on having the longest list of ex-husbands. I'm sure she would've *really* sunk her claws into your Grandpa Cal, if his eye hadn't wandered to a younger model." She flickers like an old silent movie.

"So we get the last laugh where Liliané's concerned though, right?"

Her hesitation is about to concern me, but, at last, she returns from memory lane. Grams giggles into her festooned fingers like a schoolgirl playing dress-up with her mom's jewels. "We do."

"You better make cards for Leticia Whitecloud and her goons. The fact that she was tucked safely below deck when I found her, doesn't mean she didn't give the word. There were a few other shifty characters at the private poker game, but they all seemed genuinely shocked to hear about Vassili's death."

"But was it genuine?" Grams arches an eyebrow.

"Oh, right. I keep forgetting I'm a psychic! Give me a minute." I close my eyes and replay the scene as I walked through the poker game the second time and announced the tragedy. "Yep, genuine shock. The guy who was losing big is actually excited to hear the news, but I think that was simply because he was looking for any excuse to end the game."

Isadora crosses her arms and floats up to the ceiling in quiet contemplation.

"I should probably—" At that exact moment my phone pings with a text. "It's from Erick."

Ghost-ma ignores me.

I read the text aloud anyway. He says, "Breakfast at Myrtle's? Can you manage 9:00 a.m.?"

I mumble as I type my reply. "Manage 9:00 a.m.! Who does he think he's dealing with?"

She finally responds. "I remember a young lady

who couldn't get up before noon when she first arrived on—what did you call it?—Dante's *Inferno* bus."

That old Mitzy seems like a different person. Every time I think back to my miserable hamster wheel of an existence, I feel more and more gratitude for the one-way ticket that got me straight out of it.

"*New* Mitzy can manage 9:00 a.m. And, for your information, there are some things I miss about Arizona."

"Well, I'm pretty sure it wasn't that horrible guy you occasionally hooked up with. What was his name again? You used to mumble it in your sleep all the time . . . Ben!"

"Oh boy. I forgot all about Shady Ben. I definitely don't miss him. But I do miss the monsoon season. There's something incredible about a thunderstorm in the desert. Massive cracks of lightning and a deluge of water dumping down on parched earth. It's pretty spectacular, even from a tiny window with security bars on the outside. Plus, there's a sweet smell in the air afterward that reminds me of damp railroad tracks—but uplifting."

"That sounds lovely, dear." Grams sinks down to eye level and studies the murder wall. "You don't have a connection between Leticia and Liliané."

I turn toward her. "And?"

"It's just that, back when Leticia was running things at the Hawk Island Casino, Liliané and her third husband spent four nights a week out there. I know she was a high roller, so Leticia had to be aware of her. She seems to keep anyone with money on her radar."

"Speaking from experience, Grams?"

"You know full well that it's a very bad idea for a recovering alcoholic to substitute another vice for alcohol. So, no, I didn't make a habit of it. Again, I may have ventured out once or twice, but it was purely recreational. I didn't have a gambling problem."

"Clearly. You had a husband problem. And an unspecified number of special friends problem."

Her apparition ripples with shock. "There's absolutely nothing wrong with sharing meaningful relationships with interesting men."

"Of course not. As long as there's no overlapping of those relationships." I wink at Grams. She chooses to ignore my innuendo and leave my notion unconfirmed. However, I'm astutely observant, and I've seen and heard enough subtle hints since I landed in almost-Canada to confirm my own suspicions. I inherited my inner skank straight from the trunk of the family tree.

"Well, I never!"

"We don't have time to debate that, Grams."

Pyewacket appears from the closet, in all his sleek tan glory. Either he's been taking an extremely long nap or yet another secret passage exists within my hidden apartment. He saunters out and drops something at my feet.

"Is that a toy? Do you want to play fetch?"

"Ree-ow." Soft but condescending. If I didn't know better, I'd almost think he meant "stupid human."

"Well, excuse me, Pye. What is this thing?" I reach down, pick up the object, and mindlessly shake it back and forth as I struggle to determine its identity.

Grams zips over and scrunches up her ethereal nose. "Is that a baby rattle? Why do you have a baby rattle?"

"I don't know? It's not mine. Pye brought it to me." I gesture defensively toward the spoiled feline. "Aren't cats supposedly rumored to suck the souls out of babies? Maybe he was making his rounds and took a souvenir."

"Mizithra!" Her phantom limb swings toward my backside with surprising force.

I jump forward and barely escape her retribution. "Hey! You're getting a little bit dangerous." I shake the rattle back and forth and toss it on the coffee table. "Consider it officially logged into evidence, Pyewacket."

He leaps onto my four-poster bed, spins in a circle three times, and settles into my eight-hundred-thread-count Egyptian cotton sheets. It would appear his black-tufted ears are in urgent need of cleaning, and he has no time to discuss any further information regarding my case.

CHAPTER 6

WALKING OUT THE FRONT door of my bookstore, I choose to take a small detour before heading directly to my breakfast with Sheriff Too-Hot-To-Handle. The Bell, Book & Candle sits squarely on the corner of First Avenue and Main Street. Main Street comes to a dead end in a shallow cul-de-sac beside the store, overlooking the great lake that brings so much beauty and commerce to our small town.

Humidity is a new concept for an Arizona desert girl. But one of the advantages of living this close to a massive body of water is the interesting weather patterns pushed upon us by the unpredictable wind. No matter the level of humidity, a brisk breeze across this beautiful lake does quite a bit to remove the stickiness from the air.

I glance over at the front door of the bookshop and smile. A thick wooden door intricately carved with whimsical vignettes, such as: a centaur chasing a maiden through delicate woodland; a faun playing a flute for a family of rabbits dancing around his cloven feet; the shadow of a winged horse passing in front of the moon; a wildcat stalking a small boy—a cat who bears a striking resemblance to Pyewacket.

The massive door was a grand opening gift from Silas to Grams. The singular key to the door hangs on a chain around my neck. It's a hefty brass key with a unique triangle-shaped barrel. I used to wear it around my neck every single day when I first came to Pin Cherry, but after a few undercover missions requiring low-cut tops or very tight corsets, I generally enter through the alley door using a regular-sized key.

But today I missed the weight of it around my neck and tucked it under my T-shirt. The image emblazoned across my cotton tee is a snarky little cat pushing a glass off the counter above the message, "I do what I want."

I feel like Erick and I are at a place in our seedling relationship where he can truly appreciate the depth of this sentiment.

After hustling down Main Street toward Myrtle's Diner, despite the breeze rolling in from the shore, I'm grateful for the cool blast of air conditioning that envelops me when I push open the glass door.

Odell gives me his standard spatula salute through the red-Formica-trimmed orders-up window, and I smell my delicious breakfast already sizzling on the grill.

Ever since I met him, I've been impressed with the way he seems to have a sixth sense about his regular customers' dietary needs. And he absolutely knows I *needs me* some scrambled eggs with chorizo and a side of golden-brown home fries.

The snug, flame-red bun of my favorite waitress, Tally, pops out from the kitchen, and in one smooth move she scoops up a coffee mug and fills it en route to the corner booth, which holds the true reward for my early morning rising.

Erick smiles in that way that makes my tummy tingly and warm, and as I slide onto the red-vinyl seat across from him, he steals one of my moves.

He walks his fingers across the table and turns his palm upward in a clear and enticing invitation.

Blushing, in spite of our familiarity, I eagerly place my hand in his.

He gives it a little squeeze. "Did you have that shirt custom-made?"

I'd already forgotten what I was wearing, and I

nearly spit out my first sip of delicious coffee. After a ferocious struggle, I manage to swallow the coffee and answer. "You'd think, right?"

He smiles and pulls his hand back to grip his coffee. "So your dad seemed pretty cozy with Jimmy . . ."

For a moment I struggle with the propriety of the story that my father told me, but I've seen local law enforcement go after the easy mark of an ex-con one too many times. Looks like I'll have to break my promise, in order to keep my dad off the suspect list. At least it's for a good cause. "My dad did time with Jimmy's son down at Clearwater. Story is, he saved the kid's life in the yard one day. They're not friends or anything, but Jimmy gives him prison respect or whatever you call it."

Erick's coy grin sends my extra senses into overdrive. There is an odd combination of smugness, appreciation, and surprise.

"But you already knew that."

His eyes widen. "Remind me never to play poker with you."

Shaking my head, I take another slow sip of coffee before I reply. "For your sake, I hope you never play poker in this town. We don't need another member of local law enforcement under Leticia's thumb."

Erick raises his mug of coffee. "Hear. Hear."

"When do you expect to get your hands on the medical examiner's report?"

He grins. "And there's that toss from left field I can always count on."

Odell slides our breakfasts, and a bottle of Tabasco, onto the table and raps his knuckles twice before he saunters back to the kitchen.

Our discussion is temporarily placed on hold while I douse my home fries with spicy sauce and we fill our bellies with comfort food.

"The medical examiner should have something for me this afternoon. I don't expect any surprises. Vassili was clearly strangled. All we have to do is figure out by who."

It pleases me to hear him use the word "we." "I think you mean by *whom*."

He rolls his eyes lightly and smiles. "Any hunches?"

Unsure about his tone, I launch into a defensive, "Look, mister, I've—"

"Hey, I'm a believer. I think it was you who mentioned that your hunches have solved a lot of cases since you came to town. My job is to enforce the law and see that justice is served. I don't have to be picky about how I get there."

My scrambled-egg-laden fork halts halfway to

my mouth. Either I'm having another one of my daytime hallucinations, or Sheriff Erick Harper has welcomed me aboard the investigative team.

He must sense my shock, because he chuckles softly. "You heard me right. I'm a believer."

I'm not even going to ask what he believes, or what kind of access this new belief will grant me. "Great. Then I'm going to keep doing what I do best. Stumble upon corpses, interfere with investigations, and ferret out criminals."

Erick nods his nonverbal agreement and, for a moment, I sense a wave of something close to pride rolling my way. He's proud of me. He's really proud of me.

"What are you grinning about, Moon?"

"Nothing." Painting my face in a portrait of innocence is becoming increasingly more difficult.

"Right." He shakes his head and dives back into his breakfast.

I'm not ashamed to say I finish first. Which is fine, because it gives me the opportunity to ask questions. "Who's your lead suspect right now?"

He wipes a little syrup from the corner of his mouth and licks his finger, which causes me to blush and swallow uncomfortably.

"I'd love to say it's Whitecloud and her goons, but so far there's nothing pointing at them. And you discovering her in that hidden room below deck gives her one heck of an alibi."

"Well, I'm not ruling her out. I barely know my way around that boat and I found that hidden room in under two minutes. She could easily have killed Vassili and made it back there before I discovered her."

Erick nods. "True."

I offer him my hunch. "But my favorite suspect has got to be Roman, the brother."

He tilts his head. "I thought you said in your statement that he was drinking at the bar on the main deck?"

"Oh, for sure."

Now it's Erick's turn to almost spit out his coffee and put a hand over his mouth until he regains control.

"What?"

"You're starting to sound like a local."

I reflect on my almost-Canada-style response and smirk. "Oh, yeah, I see what I did there. Anyway, back to my hunch." Wink. "I saw Roman arguing with Vassili and shoving him against the railing. Which is why he would've been even more upset if he found out that, in addition to getting all the money, Vassili was simultaneously having an affair with Iris and schtupping a waitress on his dead wife's memorial cruise."

"Schtupping?"

"Guilty." I shrug. "Foster family number five was Jewish. They were nice enough, but there was a lot of Yiddish and words like 'schtupping' that I can't seem to erase from my mind."

"Fair enough." Erick pushes his plate back and grips his coffee with his strong sexy fingers. Don't judge. It might sound strange to say fingers are sexy, but think about it. Some fingers have hairy knuckles. Some fingers are fat and sausage-y. Some fingers have hideously cared for nails. Maybe it's just me, but he's got sexy fingers.

"Mitzy? Mitzy? Am I boring you already?"

"Not likely. I drifted off into one of my mind movies."

"Is that a film-school-dropout thing?" He raises an eyebrow expectantly.

I give him a half grin and an eyelid flutter. "It's a me thing. It was a survival skill I developed after my mom passed away. When things would get too sad or too hard or too real, I would disappear into my mind. Unfortunately, the problem got worse after film school."

Erick reaches across the table, and when I slip my hand in his, he gently rubs his thumb across my fingers. "I'll never be able to really express how sorry I am that you lost your mother. But, is it wrong of me to be glad that you ended up in Pin Cherry?"

My heart swells in my chest and my rib cage feels too small to contain it. "No, it's actually kind of sweet."

He gives my hand a squeeze. "Time for me to get back to the station. You'll let me know what you find out, right?" Erick slides out of the booth and walks toward the door, giving me a perfect excuse to look over my shoulder and enjoy his exit.

"I always share my intel, Sheriff."

"How about we shoot for sharing in a *timely* manner this go-round, Moon?"

"I'll see what I can do."

His head wags from side to side, and the low rumble of his chuckle disappears as he leaves the diner.

Bussing our dishes, I place them in the dish bin behind the counter, because when you've worked in the service industry as long as I have, you know there's always a bus bin behind the counter.

I wave to Odell and say goodbye to Tally as I head back to the bookshop to study my murder wall and plan my next move.

Fortuitously, my phone rings with a call from Mr. Willoughby.

"Good morning, Silas. How may I help you?"

My extreme formality actually elicits a chuckle from Mr. Manners.

"You're at the bookshop, right—? Never mind, I see the Model T." I end the call without saying goodbye, which I know I will be admonished for, but I'm literally steps away from my shop.

My mentor's pristine 1908 Model T is parked out front. I check the main door of the bookstore and find it open. That means Twiggy is here and ready to knock me down a peg.

"Before you say anything, Silas, I'm sorry I hung up."

He harrumphs into his bushy grey mustache and smooths it with a thumb and forefinger. "Indeed."

"Privacy?" I point toward my apartment.

He nods sharply and his hangdog jowls waggle to and fro.

Walking toward the circular staircase, I'm surprised to find the "No Admittance" sign and chain hanging unhooked. "Twiggy? Twiggy, did you unhook the chain?"

Her disembodied voice drifts down from above. "Sharp as a tack, doll. I'm unloading a shipment of rare books. You should be glad I didn't hire some young punks to help me lug these boxes up the stairs. They woulda agitated Pyewacket and you'd have paid the price."

As I circle up the winding staircase, I can't resist saying, "So, *you* can leave the chain unhooked, but I can't?" I cross my arms and wait as Twiggy backs down the enormous ladder on the left arm of the mezzanine balcony.

When she reaches the bottom, she brushes some dust off her dungarees, flicks her grey pixie cut to the side and nods. "Exactly."

Throwing my hands up in the air in defeat, I walk over to the secret bookcase door, pull the candle handle, and invite Silas to follow me in.

As the door slides back, a thought pops into my head. "Can you get me a copy of the medical examiner's report for Vassili's murder?"

"I will have to handle your sudden request this afternoon. I am wanted at the Barnes estate this morning."

I make no attempt to hide my curiosity. "Why? Is someone else dead?"

"I should think not. However, according to the provisions of Liliané Barnes' will, in the event that Vassili should precede her in death, her estate would be transferred to the contingent beneficiary."

"But Vassili didn't precede her in death. He receded her, or post-ceded her—or something."

"Succeeded. However, due to the fact that he died *intestate*, Mrs. Barnes' attorney has enacted the contingent beneficiary clause. The family will, of course, protest, as they must, but the executor has asked me to come to the estate to begin the process of probate."

"You're the contingent beneficiary?" I scrunch up my nose and shake my head in confusion.

"No, I am not. But I represent the contingent beneficiaries, the Queen of Heaven Pet Cemetery and the Pin Cherry Harbor Animal Shelter."

"She left everything to the shelter and the cemetery? She's worth billions, right?"

Ghost-ma clears her throat. "I hardly think it was billions, dear."

"Grams, now is not the right time for your socialite competition."

Silas can only hear my side of the conversation, but he's a learned man, especially in the ways of Myrtle Isadora. He pulls out his alchemically altered spectacles, cleans the rose-tinted lenses, and hooks the wire arms behind his ears. Once he locates the ghost, with the assistance of his glasses, he launches into his speech. "Isadora, it was generous of Liliané to leave her funds to a worthy cause, since she has fallen out with her family. You, on the other hand, should be grateful that you were able to share your wealth with your granddaughter. Not all families are able to repair the wounds of time."

Grams' unnaturally youthful visage is fraught with indecision.

I don't have time for this detour. "Silas, you have to get me into that house. I know one of those kids is responsible for killing Vassili, and I'm sure that if I can get access to the house, I'll get a feeling."

"And how would you propose I accomplish that? You met each and every one of the family members aboard last night's gambling boat memorial service. I should hardly think they would welcome you into their estate."

"I can be your assistant. I'll wear a disguise."

I run to the closet and yank open the deep bottom drawer of the large built-in units. As I rifle through the wigs, I shout, "Grams, mousy-brown? I want to blend in. What do you think?"

Despite her existential feud, she can't resist an undercover operation. She bursts through the wall of the closet and makes a beeline for the tailored suits.

"Definitely mousy brown. Pull it back in a loose ponytail, and we'll need to find you some thick glasses. Check in that top drawer over there with the gloves."

I follow her instructions while she paws through the skirt suits.

"Tortoiseshell rims or black?"

She turns and puts a hand on her ample hip. "Let me see both."

Silas shuffles into the doorway and tilts his head. "This appears to be a drill you two have rehearsed before. However, I made no mention of an assistant when I accepted this engagement."

"Well, call and let them know if it's so important. In my experience assistants are always forgotten. It would be more believable if you just show up with me. They won't even notice me."

Silas smooths his mustache and nods thoughtfully. "Perhaps."

I shoo him out of the closet. "I've got to change. Give me five minutes."

Slipping into the positively drab grey suit and cream blouse that Grams has selected for me, I'm frankly surprised to see something so basic in her closet.

"Basic? Has the meaning of that word changed? Is that an insult?"

"I'll scold you for thought-dropping later." Expertly tugging on the wig, I push all my white hair up underneath and secure it with some bobby pins.

"Now show me the glasses."

"Tortoiseshell?" I pull them off and put on the other pair. "Or black?"

"Definitely the black. Oh, and those exceedingly cheap fake-leather pumps. That definitely completes the 'fade into the background' ensemble." She giggles.

I push the glasses on and slip my feet into the black pumps. Strutting twice around the closet, I ask, "What do you think? Does this scream assistant, or what?"

"The suit screams assistant, but the sassy personality inside is way too confident, dear. You're going to have to work on being demure and unassuming."

"Sassy? Rude." Glaring at my ghostly critic, I'm eager to prove her wrong.

Outside the closet, I hear Silas chuckling openly.

I step out with my hands gripped at my waist, rubbing my thumbs together nervously. Staring at the ground, I mumble in a soft, whispery voice with a hint of a lisp. "Yes, Mr. Willoughby. Right away, Mr. Willoughby."

This performance brings a fresh set of belly laughs to my alchemist/attorney. His face reddens dangerously and his jowls jiggle like little bags full of jelly.

"Take a deep breath, Silas. It's not permanent. It's only for today."

He leans back with a hand on his round paunch and struggles to take a deep breath. "Then this day shall be the single greatest in my personal history."

"Oh brother." I roll my eyes mercilessly behind

my stage-prop eyewear. "Do I need a briefcase, or clipboard?"

Silas appraises my outfit. "You do indeed look the part. I tell you what, I shall allow you to carry my briefcase."

"Glory be." I raise my hands in false praise.

Silas heads toward the secret door, and I follow without being asked.

He presses the intricate plaster medallion, and as the door slides open—

Ghost-ma cries out, "What's your name?"

"Grams, are you all right? I'm Mitzy. You know my name."

Before she can reply, Silas interjects. "Not to overstep, and I realize I did not hear the actual query, but could your grandmother possibly have made a reference to your cover identity?"

"Oh, right. Let's see, I've used Daisy, and Darcy . . . How about Dora? Dora seems like an unmemorable name, right?"

Grams chuckles. "Well, I suppose not to someone actually named Dora. But it'll work. Last name? I don't think it's right for Silas to refer to his assistant by her first name."

"Donaldson. Dora Donaldson."

Silas nods. "Follow me, Ms. Donaldson."

It's only when we step out the front door of the

bookshop that I realize I'll have to ride in the Model T. Not the pinnacle of comfort or speed.

Begrudgingly, I climb into the mint condition 1908 Model T. The seats show some wear and the steering wheel has two smooth indentations that cradle his hands, but other than that the vehicle looks like it rolled off the assembly line yesterday.

CHAPTER 7

Smash cut to— the imposing perimeter of the Barnes estate. We reach the black iron gates that loom over our vehicle, and a large shield spanning both halves of the gate bears a Latin phrase that I don't recognize.

Silas presses the intercom and announces our arrival. As the gates swing open, I ask, "What does that Latin gibberish mean?"

"Latin is not gibberish. Mizith—"

"Dora Donaldson, Silas. Ms. Donaldson."

"Indeed, Ms. Donaldson. *Divide et Impera*. Divide and Conquer."

"What a horrible family motto. No wonder they all hate each other."

The long drive travels through manicured lawns, trimmed and snipped to within an inch of their lives. When we pull up in front of the grand entrance, a doorman steps out, holds the door with a gloved hand, and stands absolutely still, refusing to make any eye contact, as we mount the stairs.

Before we make it through the doorway, I'm hit with the thick odor of stale tobacco smoke. *Thank You for Smoking!* The local dive bar, Final Destination, smells better than this.

Inside, the great hall opens onto a vast black-and-grey marble floor, with a seven-tiered crystal chandelier dominating the high ceiling. A grand staircase, carpeted in deep red, opens before us and divides in opposite directions at the first landing. On that landing stands a man I don't recognize from the viewing or the memorial cruise.

"Good morning, Mr. Willoughby, so good of you to come. Please follow me to the library."

Silas and I climb the stairs, and I take the opportunity to whisper under my breath, "See, no mention of the assistant."

Silas harrumphs, but makes no reply.

"I'm Mr. Everett. The executor. We spoke on the phone."

"How good to meet you, Mr. Everett."

Upon reaching the second floor, we march down a lengthy hallway adorned with stunning artwork.

My mentor never misses an opportunity. "Ms.

Donaldson, allow us to slow our pace. This is a rare treat." He gestures to the individual masterpieces. "Matisse. Rousseau. An immaculate Cézanne. Those are both by Toulouse-Lautrec. Van Gogh. And an unmistakable Paul Gauguin." He ceases his recitation and addresses our guide. "Is the entire collection Post-Impressionists?"

"Ah, yes. You have a keen eye." Mr. Everett nods his admiration.

I stare in wonder at the works. I mean, the frames alone seem as though they would be worth a fortune. In addition to the paintings and sketches, there's a full suit of armor in the hallway, several marble busts, and even a marble statue of the Madonna and Child.

The fascinating art show ends as we walk through a gilded archway into a library three times the size of Mr. Willoughby's, and nearly as large as the Bell, Book & Candle.

Violet, Roman, Iris, and her husband sit on the opposite side of a massive oak table, each of them looking much the worse for wear.

Violet still has streaks of smeared mascara under her eyes and her plump skin is an unhealthy ashen hue.

Roman is smoking, and the ashtray in front of him would indicate he's mowed through half a pack, waiting for our arrival. He certainly bears some portion of the responsibility for the wretched smell clinging to the walls. Although, I can't believe he's allowed to smoke near such priceless artwork.

Iris does not look up. Her hands continue to fidget in her lap, while her husband tightens the protective arm already around her muscular shoulders.

This is honestly the first time I've taken any notice of the husband. He's much older than his late-thirties bride, has obvious hair plugs, and his eyes scream, "We've been tucked one too many times."

Mr. Everett gestures to two of the rolling wooden chairs on our side of the table. "Please have a seat. Do you care for water, Mr. Willoughby?"

I'm about to mention that I'd like some water, but I remember I'm a mousy unassuming assistant and wisely keep my mouth shut.

Silas for the win. "Yes. Two waters would be most appreciated, Mr. Everett."

The executor gestures to a servant who had been standing in the corner, and, let's be honest, had completely escaped my notice.

He then opens his thick leather folio and begins going over the extraordinarily boring preamble to Liliané's will. "I won't reread the personal gifts and family heirlooms. There shall be no change in those bequests. However, the estate, the art collection, the grounds, the vineyards, and all of Liliané's liquid assets are to be divided 30/70 between the Queen of Heaven Pet Cemetery and the Pin Cherry Harbor Animal Shelter."

Roman throws his half-smoked cigarette on the carpet and shoves his chair back in anger.

Violet screams and stamps out the cigarette butt.

Iris turns and buries her head in her husband's chest, as her shoulders shake with sobs.

Her sorrow has nothing to do with her departed mother. My special gifts indicate her anguish is one hundred and ten percent in response to the loss of her inheritance.

Roman storms out of the library, muttering un-repeatable epithets under his breath about his re-cently deceased mother, Euro-trash, and filthy animals defecating on his birthright.

Violet puts her hand over her tiny, rosebud mouth, and, even with the help of my extra senses, I can't quite tell if she's offended or about to be sick.

She runs out whimpering.

Mr. Everett takes it all in stride. "Iris, do you have any questions for Mr. Willoughby?"

"Just one." Her sharp features pinch in disdain. "How can you live with yourself?"

Silas smooths his mustache and replies, "Were you and your mother close, Mrs. Barnes-Becker?"

Unfortunately for poor Iris she has no idea who she's dealing with. But I have the advantage of knowing that when Silas answers a question with a question, he's about to serve up a lesson.

Mr. Becker steps in to defend his wife. "I'm not sure what business it is of yours."

"It may, in fact, not be my business, Mr. Becker. However, your wife asked me a question and I feel I am duty-bound to respond."

Iris stares quizzically at Silas. "Everyone in this town knows my mother and I had a falling out. That doesn't mean she has the right to cut me out of the will. I paid my dues. I was born in this house, grew up in this house, endured her endless insults in this house. I deserve compensation."

This time, she makes no attempt to hide her tears.

Silas nods compassionately. "I wonder, would you have any interest in serving on the board of the Pin Cherry Harbor Animal Shelter?"

Her head snaps up and my initial read of her energy pulses with negativity. But as a light flickers in her eyes, I can feel her whole essence shift. "I could do that. I like animals."

"Very well. I shall put a motion before the board at our next meeting. Perhaps you would entertain the use of the Barnes manor as a permanent fundraising location for the shelter and other non-profits in town. We would, of course, require a full-time caretaker to live on the property, and see to the day-to-day affairs here. This position would come with compensation."

For a split-second Iris emits a flicker of pleased energy, which rapidly shifts towards guilt.

I'd like to know if that guilt is solely connected to her affair with Vassili, or if there's more to it. Time to snoop. I lean toward Silas and whisper, "I need to use the restroom, Mr. Willoughby."

He nods. "Mr. Everett, would you be kind enough to point my assistant toward the nearest lavatory?"

"Of course. Follow me, Miss."

Stepping out of the library, he gestures down the long hallway. "And then you'll make a left, go down three doors, and the Cerulean Bath will be on your right."

Bowing my head in an awkward partial curtsy, I shuffle down the hall, turn the corner, and, once I'm out of sight, lean up against the wall next to a marble bust of Shakespeare on a pedestal. I whisper into the stone ear of the somewhat-disputed king of tragedies, "Violet and Roman are not going to be happy when they find out about the deal that Iris struck."

And before I can enter the Cerulean Bath, an icy chill sweeps down the corridor and goosebumps rise on my arms.

All of my senses, the regular and the extra ones, are on high alert. I dive into the bathroom and close the door.

But right behind me something bursts through the door.

And I mean *through* the door. Through the closed door!

"Liliané?"

The swirling mist coalesces and definitely resembles the woman whose face I saw in the casket a little more than twenty-four hours ago.

"You can see me?"

"Apparently."

She exhales dramatically and fans herself with one hand. "Fantastic, darling. I'll take a dry martini, dirty, two olives."

"You know you can't actually drink a martini, right?"

"Don't lecture me! I'm Liliané Barnes! If I can have a martini delivered to the top of the Eiffel Tower, I can certainly have one in my own home. Now, scoot!"

"I mean, you can't drink a martini because you're dead." I cross my arms and raise one eyebrow.

"How inconvenient, darling. Are you sure?"

"Positive."

"We'll bump that up to your supervisor later. At least someone can see and hear me. Now we can get to the bottom of things."

"Get to the bottom of what?"

"My murder, of course."

CHAPTER 8

A SMALL PORTION of my shock and awe can be attributed to seeing a ghost other than Grams, but the majority is hanging on this one's last words. "I'm sorry, your what?"

"My murder. Are you hard of hearing as well as poorly dressed?"

I sincerely hope this ghost can't hear my thoughts, because I'm starting to get a real feel for why her children are estranged! "Oh, I heard you. Except, according to the official report, you died of natural causes. There was no autopsy and no suspicion of foul play. And your family physician said you had a long history of emphysema and died in your sleep of respiratory complications."

Liliané crosses her arms haughtily and scoffs.

"You seem to have a lot of information for a lowly assistant. What's your story?"

Shrugging my shoulders, I dive in. "Since there's not a lot of people you can tell, I'll give it to you straight, Mrs. Barnes. I'm a psychic. I'm Isadora Duncan's granddaughter—"

The grande dame of Barnes manor sighs and rolls her eyes. "Of course. Even in death that woman is spying on me."

Ignoring her poke at my family tree, I continue, "As I was saying, I inherited her bookshop, and I'm a pretty good amateur sleuth. I'm actually here, undercover, investigating Vassili's murder."

This information rocks her world, and the all-too-familiar translucent ghost tears that leak from her eyes give me a surge of guilt.

"Sorry. I thought you would know. Isn't his ghost on the other side with you?"

She angrily swipes her tears away and once again looks down her ethereal nose at me. "For a psychic, you don't seem to know very much about the afterlife, darling. Clearly, I'm trapped here in this mansion because I have unfinished business. I had no idea my gorgeous Vassili had crossed over. Poor little lamb."

There's way too much to unpack in that tirade, so I choose to back up to the information that's actually important. "We can debate the finer points of extrasensory perception at a later date. You claim you were murdered. What evidence do you have, and why should I care?"

Her eyes widen. Obviously she's not used to being spoken to as an equal. "The cheek of you. Do you have any idea who I am?"

Time to knock this ghost down a peg. "Of course I do. You're the utterly powerless ghost of a woman who lived her life so completely self-involved that none of her three children even mourn her passing."

"Powerless, eh." Liliané swirls into an angry mist and surges toward me.

I instinctively put my hands up over my face, as if that can stop a ghost from passing through me, but, after a moment of anticipation with no consequences, I crack open my eyelids and peer around the bathroom. "Liliané? Was there gonna be a demonstration?"

A whimpering sound causes me to turn toward the tub. And there, sulking on the edge of an enormous blue-glass bathtub, is the defeated ghost of Liliané Barnes.

"You're right. You're absolutely right. I am utterly powerless. I've tried to move objects. Tried to leave this place. Tried to frighten my children. But no one can see me. I can't move anything. I can't intimidate anyone."

It's difficult for me to imagine my greatest regret after death being the inability to intimidate someone, but far be it from me to want to live in this poor woman's world. "Look, I'm sorry to be so harsh. If you really were murdered, I'll absolutely help you. It's kind of my thing." I lean down and attempt to pat her shoulder.

She jerks away. "What are you doing?"

"Apparently, making the horrible mistake of attempting to comfort you."

"Why would you be kind to me?"

"I learned the hard way that everyone deserves a second chance. Plus, I lost my mom when I was eleven, and I actually loved her."

Liliané brushes her bleached grey-blonde hair back from her face. "I may have made a few mistakes as a mother, but I amassed a fortune and a singular collection of fine art. Not to mention, I still hold the record for most ex-husbands north of the Mason-Dixon."

There's no time for all the counseling this diva needs. "Let's try to stay on topic. I've got to get back to the library before they start to think there's something seriously wrong with my digestive tract. Why do you think you were murdered?"

"Simple, darling. I woke up to grab a ciggy and found a pillow smashed over my face. I struggled and thrashed, but whoever was shoving the pillow down was stronger than me. He or she just kept pushing that pillow tighter and tighter, until I couldn't get air in my—"

"There's no need to finish, I believe you Liliané. But I need more time to search the house, question your children, look into your affairs."

"How did you know I was having an affair?"

"Having a what now?"

"Oh, were you referring to my financial affairs? Never mind."

Note to self: This family is full of lechers, and did she say a cigarette? With emphysema? Unbelievable. "I need more time. How do I get back into the house? Legitimately?"

"What day is it?"

"Saturday. Why?"

She swirls around the bathroom, fluffing her hair and dabbing a finger under each eye. "Let's see, tomorrow is Sunday. Oh, Upstairs Maid has Sundays off, darling. Show up tomorrow at 8:00 a.m. Come in through the servants' entrance and take a maid's uniform from the closet. You'll have free access to the house for at least eight hours. Sometimes Upstairs Maid works ten hours . . . That should give you enough time."

This woman is a real piece of work. "And no one will be suspicious that *Upstairs Maid* looks like a completely different person and came to work on Sunday?"

"Oh dear, you really are a blue-collar girl. No one even knows Upstairs Maid's name. I doubt very seriously they've noticed what she looks like. You'll be fine."

Before this is all over, I will figure out how to punch a ghost squarely in the face. "Perfect. Looks like you found yourself a new upstairs maid."

She checks her fingernails and sighs. "I don't suppose you have any references?"

"You can't be serious?"

"Well, one can't be too careful."

"Listen, Liliané, I'm going to help you, but don't misinterpret that to mean I like you. I'd advise you not to push your luck with me. In the meantime, why don't you make yourself useful and listen in on any conversations that seem suspicious or secretive. You might not be able to scare anyone—poor you—but you can definitely eavesdrop. All right?"

"How gauche." She wipes a manicured hand across her creaseless brow. "If you insist."

"I do. Now I have to get back."

Hurrying down the long hallway, which I'm nicknaming Passageway of the Masters, I find the library empty of Liliané's offspring.

Silas raises one bushy eyebrow and I subtly shake my head.

Mr. Everett stands. "Let me walk you out, Mr. Willoughby."

"You're too kind." Silas hands me his briefcase and I take it with a sigh.

We head back through the grand mansion, down the wide carpeted staircase, and across the polished marble floor.

"I'll be in touch with Iris about the board's decision."

"Such a generous offer, Mr. Willoughby. Perhaps more generous than she deserves."

Despite the superficial gratitude of the statement, my clairaudience picks up an entirely different phrase. Mr. Everett is actually thinking that Iris is the least deserving and most conniving of the children.

Silas opens the car door for me.

Taking a moment to suck down a gulp of fresh, non-ashtray-scented air, I slip into the Model T and wait impatiently while he goes through the lengthy cranking startup process.

Once we're trundling back toward Pin Cherry proper, I spill my story.

"So, Lilian é was murdered. Her ghost is haunting the house. And she sort of hired me to solve the case."

Silas laughs openly. "And here I was assuming you were experiencing possible digestive discordance."

"For the record, she's as awful as everyone says."

Silas grins. "Not the first I've heard." He taps his thumb against the steering wheel. "Will you be keeping me abreast of your plan?"

"What makes you think I have a plan?"

He takes his eyes off the road long enough to blast me with a scathing look.

"All right. There's a plan." I fill him in on the details as we drive to the bookshop.

He turns down the alleyway between the Duncan Restorative Justice Foundation and my bookstore. "My apologies, but I am unable to stay, Mitzy. I must complete my correspondence to the bequeathed charities before the end of the day. You'll bring your grandmother up to speed?"

"Of course. I'm sure she'll want me to run a subversive mission to gather dirt on Liliané while I'm in the enemy's camp." I chuckle as I exit the vehicle.

Silas leans across and his wise, milky-blue eyes fix me with an unreadable gaze. "Your grandmother may yet surprise you." And with that he reverses out of the alley and disappears.

Twiggy is nowhere to be found, and the chain is securely fastened across the bottom of the circular staircase. But, to test my theory, I unhook the chain, step onto the first tread, and wait.

Silence.

She's definitely not here.

Hooking the chain behind me, I march into my apartment, struggling to remove my bobby pins and the now itchy wig. "Grams? Grams, do you want to hear the plan or not?"

Another round of silence.

Where is everyone? Doesn't she want to hear what I did?

Pyewacket pushes himself to a seated position on the large four-poster bed and stretches one paw to the side, almost as though he's resting it on his hip. "Don't *you* want to hear what *I* did?"

My Bladder Control 101 training comes in handy, but I can't stop my jaw from dropping. "Robin Pyewacket Goodfellow, did you actually *speak* to me?"

"Oh, Mitzy. You should've seen your face, dear."

My mouth is still hanging open and I can't figure out what I'm seeing. Pyewacket's head is bobbing back and forth and his jaw is moving as though he's speaking to me.

"Grams? Is that you? Are you working Pyewacket like a ventriloquist dummy?"

"In a manner of speaking. I think I've successfully possessed him."

A shock ripples across my skin, and I can't believe what I'm hearing. "Get out of that cat! You have completely crossed the line, Isadora. That sentient animal can't give his consent." I rush toward Pyewacket and, as soon as my left arm scoops around him and my magicked mood ring touches his skin, the apparition of my grandmother bolts out of my precious fur baby.

Pyewacket cuddles against me, and I've honestly never seen him act so helpless or afraid.

"Grams, what's gotten into you? It's not like you to treat Pyewacket so disrespectfully. Is something wrong? I mean, really wrong?"

She blows across the apartment like an angry storm cloud and sinks onto the scalloped-backed chair. "Three more rejection letters today."

"What are you talking about? I feel like you've dropped me into one of those *Memento*-style movies that use backward storytelling to reveal the twist. Who was rejected and from what?"

She throws her head back and lays a misty forearm dramatically across her brow. "The publishers. They rejected my memoirs."

The hairs on the back of my neck spike. "How would they even know about your memoirs? You didn't start writing them until after you were dead."

She sighs and smooths the folds of her Marchesa gown. "I wrote the query letters, dear. I sent out nearly thirty in the last two or three months. I can't be sure. Time has so little meaning."

"You're writing letters from beyond the grave? Don't you think that's the reason you're getting rejected? If these publishers have half a brain, they would definitely look up the name of the author. Seeing that the author is *dead*, I'm assuming that's why they're rejecting the manuscript. But I'd be happy to give it a read if you want some notes."

"Notes? From a girl who barely has more than twenty years on this planet? I think not. You do know what a life I've led, right?"

"Grams, this is so not you. I get that you're upset about the rejections, but you might have to send out a hundred letters or maybe even two hundred letters before you find the right publisher."

"They don't know who they're dealing with. I once had a martini delivered to the top of the Eiffel Tower."

The hands that were busily consoling Pyewacket fall still. "That's the second time I've heard that story today." I narrow my gaze and study Ghost-ma.

A guilty flash of self-consciousness spins through my grandmother's translucent eyes. "You don't say. Who else told you that story? Silas?"

"The ghost of Liliané Barnes. And in her version, she ordered the martini."

Grams rockets across the room. "What? Now she's a ghost? That woman will never get tired of imitating me. How does she look? Did she choose a younger age? Is she younger than me?"

"Good grief. If I never see this side of you again, it'll be too soon." I roll my eyes far longer than necessary. "Are you saying she stole the story from you? Because I'm supposed to work at her mansion tomorrow and investigate her murder, so I'd kinda like to know if she's a con artist."

"Oh, she's a con artist. I think she's a little more than that, but I could never get absolute proof." Grams swirls around, lost in a fog of memories.

Unfortunately, I have to interrupt. "Is it your story or hers?"

"Both."

"You're going to have to expand on that, Missy."

"I met Liliané, back when she was Lillian, while Max and I were drinking our way across Europe. You remember Max, dear, my second husband?"

I nod. "I'm familiar."

"Well, Max and I were all about parties, booze, gambling, and buying our way into the upper crust across the pond. Lillian seemed to be a few steps ahead of us and she took an immediate liking to Max. She invited us onto a yacht in the Mediterranean for a couple of weeks and then we all headed to France, via Italy. She would disappear for a few days here and there, and she mentioned she had a lot of family back in the states. She was always sending gifts and packages, but when we reached Paris—things came to a head."

She pauses to collect her thoughts, and Pyewacket climbs onto my lap, spilling off either side of the ample platform.

"Everything started out glorious, as things always do in Paris. We stood at the top of the Eiffel Tower and I mused about how fantastic it would be to sip martinis as the sun set. With a snap of her fingers Lillian made it happen. And one martini led to five, and I woke up in the belly of a rowboat floating in the Seine, with no sign of Max."

Grams shakes her head. "He turned up about an hour later, stinking of her expensive French perfume. He had espresso, croissants, and a sack full of excuses." She dusts her hands a couple times, as though she's brushing off some flour. "That was the end of my friendship with Lillian, and it's ultimately what pushed me over the edge, with booze, and led to the accident that took Max's life and, as you know, one of my kidneys."

"You ran with quite a crowd, Isadora."

"Yes, and at quite a cost, dear. Max wasn't the love of my life, but he was wild, free, and oh so handsome."

I'm unable to suppress a snicker. "And we all know how sad it is when handsome people die."

She picks up a coaster from the coffee table and hurls it teasingly in my direction. "Mitzy! You're too much."

Her laughter eases the tension and I go for the jugular. "Grams, you owe Pyewacket an apology."

She slips across the room, tears streaming down her face, and kneels at the edge of the bed. "Mr. Cuddlekins, can you ever forgive me? I had no right. And I'm deeply sorry for abusing your trust."

"Re-ow." Thank you.

"I wouldn't have forgiven her so easily, Pye. But you're your own man."

He bangs his head against my shoulder and purrs affectionately.

I ruffle his ear tufts. "Now, that everything's mended in our family, let's dive into the Barnes disaster."

Grams and I spend a few hours discussing the husbands, the siblings, the enemies, and the help, and the possible suspects in both murder cases.

"You better choose a new wig for tomorrow. I agree that people rarely notice the help, but I think something with bangs will seal the deal."

Leave it to my frustrated writer of a grandmother to always expand the scene.

"What about the shoes? I definitely can't wear

my high-tops, and Liliané didn't mention anything about shoes in that servants' closet."

Grams shakes her head and lifts her hands helplessly. "It's not the kind of thing I would buy. You might have to run to the mall in Broken Rock."

"Copy that." I give Pyewacket's head one last playful scratch and grab some cash off my nightstand. "Someone will publish your memoirs, Grams. You're a fascinating woman. Twice the woman Liliané could ever be. Don't give up, all right?"

She floats toward me, and the comfort of her non-corporeal arms encircling me is indescribable.

"I love you, Grams."

"I love you too, dear."

CHAPTER 9

THE AFTERNOON WINDS ARE FIERCE, and the great lake looks as dangerous as legend would have it. Huge waves crash against the shore and a handful of sailboats race across the curve of the horizon.

A quick search on my phone for shoe stores in Broken Rock produces less than a handful of results. I tap the nearest one and hope to find a quick solution to my footwear dilemma.

On my way, I pass the statuary company I visited last winter and make an impulsive left turn. I came here months ago and found a beautiful stone cardinal that I had planned to take to my grandmother's grave. But I somehow lost my nerve and left without purchasing it. I couldn't bear to look at her headstone and process all of those emotions.

Things are different now and it feels like a healthy step.

I walk into the indoor retail area, tucked within the vast sea of stone deer, gargoyles, and angels, and retrace my steps.

My mood ring tingles on my left hand, and I see an image of the little bird. As I round the corner at the end of an aisle, the actual stone cardinal is perched on the shelf where I left him all those months ago.

Scooping him up, I foolishly stroke the little spike on his rocky head.

He's been waiting for me. It's a sign. And I know signs.

I hurry to the register, pay for my purchase, and lay the cardinal on the floormat on the passenger side of the Mercedes.

Finding a simple pair of white canvas tennis shoes proves easier than I had hoped. And on the way back to Pin Cherry an idea forms.

Maybe I should go to the cemetery today. I don't really want to tell Grams I'm going, and if I drive back to the bookstore right now, I won't be able to stop myself from thinking about the little bird and my "not so secret" plan.

Lucky for me Pin Cherry is not that large and we only have one cemetery—for humans, that is.

I pull into the funerary grounds and my heart cracks a little.

There's a small group gathered under an awning, next to a mound of fresh earth.

Death is never easy. Whether it's expected or it hits out of the blue and turns your life upside down, it always hurts. It's always hard.

My eyes are already rimmed with tears and I haven't even found her gravesite.

Parking my car, I walk to the office, but it's locked. Either it's closed for the day, or the sole caretaker is out amongst the stones.

Clutching the cardinal to my chest, I close my eyes, take a deep breath, and let my psychic senses lead me.

At first my own fears block my gifts. I suppose I'm afraid that if I reach out too freely, some of the restless souls in the graveyard will grab on.

I have to risk it.

Hopefully, if I hold an image of my grandmother in my heart, I can use some of that *focus* Silas is always talking about to find the one thing I actually want.

Taking a deep breath, I call to mind the loving face of Grams. My footsteps falter for a moment or two, but then my strides become more sure. I walk confidently, as though I'm following a path I've walked down many times before.

Striding between the rows of headstones and statuary, I turn left and then right, before climbing a small hill, and making one final right.

Unexpectedly, a feeling of unconditional love, tainted by sadness, washes over me.

Her headstone is twice the size it needs to be, in order to contain all of her names.

I kneel and lovingly touch the fresh flowers the caretaker must've placed in the vase below her tombstone earlier today. I set the stone cardinal on the plinth and trace my finger along the letters carved into the cold marble.

Sadness floods through me.

Swallowing with difficulty, I exhale the pain.

A sense of relief washes over me and lightens my heart.

Yes, for all practical purposes, Isadora is dead. But I'm happy to say that in my life she lives on.

Sitting carefully on the well-manicured lawn, I lean against the headstone and close my eyes. In the quiet, my mind wanders to my mother.

Maybe I can use my psychic senses to replay some memory of my mother's funeral.

There's certainly the horrible gut-wrenching ache that followed the message my poor babysitter was forced to deliver. But I've always had that memory.

My special abilities didn't manifest until after I

arrived in Pin Cherry and placed my grandmother's mood ring on my finger.

Maybe I can't use those powers to enhance memories of things that happened before I technically had the gifts.

But I can't even recall a regular memory.

Everything after the babysitter telling me my mother had died in a terrible accident is a blur. The next thing I remember is sitting in the passenger seat of my caseworker's car as he drove me to foster family number one.

Maybe the trauma is blocking the memories. It's not all that important anymore. Maybe one day, if I feel strongly enough, I'll seek out a hypnotherapist or something to see if I can reach through the trauma and regain the memories. However, I'm sure the images would be terrible, and I'm probably better off without them.

I kiss the little spiky head of the stone cardinal, inhale the scent of the fresh freesias, and touch my grandmother's name one more time.

"I'm glad you found your way to me, Isadora." When I stand and wipe an errant tear from my cheek, I realize I have no idea where I am.

The funerary grounds are larger than I remember.

There was a hill involved. Let's retrace my steps.

I trudge down the hill, and, at the bottom, I can see around the large oak tree next to the small awning on the other side of the cemetery.

Now that I have my bearings, I walk back to my car and drive home. And it really is home. It's the first place that I've lived, without my mother, that I've actually felt I could call home.

I can't possibly know what the future is for me in Pin Cherry Harbor, but the present is more than I ever thought I deserved.

The sun is sinking low on the horizon, and the lavender and orange streaks in the sky are mirrored in the great body of water.

Tonight seems like a night to order pizza, share stories with Grams, and get to bed early.

No part of me is looking forward to rising at the crack of dawn or being a maid at the Barnes house of horrors, but I am a little bit fired up to do some proper investigating.

CHAPTER 10

WHOEVER SAID, "The early bird catches the worm," had a very high opinion of worms. Even Pyewacket is uninterested in rising at the unholy hour 6:30 a.m.

Stumbling downstairs and pouring Fruity Puffs for a cat who hasn't even gotten out of bed, has to be a new low. I'm not sure why I am worrying about being a servant to some entitled rich snobs. I'm clearly already indentured to a pompous feline.

However, his absence from the back room allows me to eat several handfuls of cereal without judgment. I hit the brew button on the coffee maker and shuffle upstairs to the shower.

The hot water and eucalyptus soap do help to pry open my eyelids.

By the time I exit the steamy retreat, Grams has placed a short black wig, with bangs, on the vanity.

"Can I put a wig over wet hair?"

"I wouldn't recommend it, dear."

"Copy that. I'll grab a cup of coffee, a quick blow-dry, and be on my way."

"Maybe a little mascara and lip tint? You know, to look professional."

"I thought you said no one notices the help, so why on earth would I need mascara and lip tint?"

"It's just— I'm afraid that— I don't want Liliané to think I raised you wrong."

"And there it is." I shake my head. "Guess what? I'm going to wear mascara and lip tint, not because I want to, but because you asked."

Grams floats down and kisses the top of my damp head. "World's best granddaughter."

"Obviously."

The steaming mug of coffee kickstarts my engine, and I am "wigged up" and out of the house in fifteen minutes.

My Jeep will definitely be the vehicle of the day, because no one in their right mind is going to believe that a maid drives a 1957 Mercedes 300SL coupe with gullwing doors.

As I near the intimidating front gates, I experience a moment of uncertainty. Liliané didn't say anything about announcing myself at the front gate. Not to mention, I don't even have a name to give!

Maybe there's a secret back entrance, like Silas has at his place. I drive past the huge shield with its horrible motto and beg my mood ring for help.

Much to my surprise, there's a subtle tingle and an image appears of a forked tree.

Up ahead on my left, the tree comes into view, and beyond it is an unassuming dirt road.

Making the left, I drive with as much confidence as an undercover snoop who doesn't know where she's going can muster.

Before long, the back of the manor looms into view. It's not nearly as impressive as the grand front entrance, but it still looks like a mini-museum.

Parking by the rest of the blue-collar cars, I fortunately see a young man enter the house through a small grey door.

The dark-haired reflection in my rearview mirror surprises me.

"What's your name?"

The face framed by a sharp black bob and perfect bangs, bats her eyelashes and says, "May as well use 'Dora,' since no one asked for a first name yesterday."

I nod my approval. In this wig I look like a Dora, *Dora the Explorer!* Except today, "Swiper" might actually be doing some swiping.

Sighing loudly, I exit my vehicle and walk through the grey door.

To my right is a white wooden door with a black sign that actually says, "Servants' Closet." Chuckling as I push through, I grab a maid's uniform that's hopefully my size.

There aren't any changing rooms in the closet, so I reenter the main hallway and take my chances with the first door on the left.

Good news. There are no naked men in here, so there's a greater than fifty percent chance that I'm in the women's room.

I step into a stall, change into my little black dress with white apron, and step out to tie the white headpiece around my wig.

Phone goes in the pocket of my apron.

Street clothes get stuffed into one of the cubbies.

Now, since I'm the new upstairs maid, I should probably go *upstairs*.

There's a back stairway that must be meant specifically for servants, so I march on up.

Three steps from the second floor, I'm forced to stop.

A severe-looking little woman in a matronly dress, with her hair piled in an elaborate grey pouf on the top of her head, stands on the landing. Her arms are crossed and her face carries a scowl for me. "And you are?"

Oh no! I can feel it happening before the words come out. The majority of my television exposure to servants has been via the BBC. I'll blame them for what is about to happen. I'm definitely going to be British and, due in no small part to the influence of *My Fair Lady*, I'm probably going to be Cockney. "Name's Dora, m'arm."

The stern woman's expression softens microscopically. "I see. And your surname?"

Dagnabbit. Think. Think. Think. "Yes, m'arm Dora Don—" Don't say Donaldson. Don't say Donaldson. "Donner."

She tilts her head skeptically and the wattle under her chin stretches. "Dora Don Donner?"

"Just Donner, m'arm." I curtsy for some unknown reason. "It's my first day, m'arm. I'm a bit strung up."

"And who hired you, Dora?"

"Mr. Barnes, m'arm." There's no way she can check that story.

"Well, Mr. Barnes has passed unexpectedly. So, I'm afraid you'll have to impress me. The upstairs maid has today off, so why don't you see if you can do a better job than her lazy, skulking behind. Lunch is at one, in the servants' kitchen. You will have thirty minutes. I will review your work throughout the day."

And my knees feel the need to give yet another curtsy. "Yes, m'arm."

She marches past me with obvious disdain, but I have no time to impress this woman.

Struggling with the vast hallways and innumerable rooms, I eventually find my way back to the Cerulean Bath. Closing the door behind me, I call out quietly, "Liliané? Liliané, it's me, Mitzy."

Nothing.

Great. My ghostly employer is AWOL and I have no idea where to begin.

Oh wait, I'm psychic. I'll start at one end and work my way through the house until something sends me a message.

A manservant is scurrying soundlessly down the hall as I step out of the bathroom.

Before I speak, I have to remind myself I'm Cockney. "Beg pardon, can you tell me where to find the maid's cupboard?"

He glides to a halt and rolls his eyes. "First day?"

"Yes, sir."

"You don't have to be formal with me, but lay it on thick when those gold-digging kids are around. Follow me."

Boy, he's no fan of the family.

He leads me to a small alcove, opens a dark creaking door and points to the many tools of my trade. "Here's your stuff. Knock yourself out. Lunch is at one, don't be late. They literally pack the food up at exactly 1:30."

"Cheers."

He hurries off to his own duties, and I grab a classic feather duster.

Starting with the first room on the left side of the hallway, I walk in and dust. I'm halfway through the room, and have opened three bureau drawers and two desk drawers, when I notice a lump under the covers in the middle of the bed.

Clapping a hand over my mouth before I can scream, I take stock. The well-muscled bare leg poking out on the far side looks male, and I'm fairly certain that's a bit of red hair peeking above the top edge of the sheet. Must be Roman.

He hasn't seemed to notice my presence, so I keep right on dusting. When I pick up his phone with my left hand, my mood ring gives me an icy jolt.

The shock causes me to drop the phone. Fortunately it lands on the carpet. The image in my mood ring is of the *Jewel of the Harbor*.

Before I can pick up the phone and attempt to generate some additional information, Roman stirs.

I hustle out of the room and quietly pull the

door closed behind me. At the next room, I knock loudly before entering.

No reply.

Opening the door, I check the bed first. This room is legitimately empty. I move through the room, checking drawers and wardrobes, but there is no information here. This one's probably been empty for some time.

As I turn to leave, I'm met with the steely gaze of the woman from the landing. "Your job is to clean, Dora, not snoop."

Joke's on her. Liliané hired me specifically to snoop. But it's time to throw on some Cockney charm. "Beg pardon, m'arm. I weren't sure if the room be occupied, m'arm." I hope, for both our sakes, that she's watched less British television than me.

"This room has been empty for some time. Dust the surfaces and move on."

This time I simply curtsy and forgo a verbal response. Feather duster in hand, I'm hard at work as her receding footsteps echo down the hall.

Peeking out the doorway, I see her turn the corner, and I make my way to room number three.

KNOCK. KNOCK. KNOCK.

No answer.

This time I close the door behind me. I'm sure

I'll get a lecture for that, but at least I'll have some warning if she checks in on me again.

Enter the room. Check bed. Snoop.

This room also appears to have been vacant for some time and my unrewarded sneakiness is growing restless.

Checking the medicine cabinet in the bathroom, I notice several herbal powders and five or six various tinctures. The labels look homemade.

So, someone in the family considers themselves a bit of an herbalist. And there must be an impressive garden on the grounds.

As I close the cabinet, an icy chill fills the room and fractals of frost creep across the glass.

I turn and smile. "Impressive. You seem to be learning new tricks with each passing day, Liliané."

She materializes in the doorway, arms crossed, with a smug look on her face. "I scared the living daylights out of Iris this morning, darling. It was absolutely fabulous."

"So who's the herbalist?"

"Why do you ask, darling?"

"All of these preparations, tinctures, and powders in the medicine cabinet. Where did they come from?"

"My fifth husband was a world-renowned botanist. Herbalism was simply a hobby. He traveled to the ends of the earth collecting specimens, cataloging species, and experimenting with preparations. In the end, one of his own experiments took his life, but for him that was the ultimate death. A beautiful sacrifice for his work. Nonsense, if you ask me."

"I need to check the girls' rooms. When do they normally vacate?"

This question brings a lengthy and forced laugh from Liliané. "Violet suffers from insomnia. She's up most of the night and sleeps until early afternoon. Iris was up at dawn and left the house without breakfast, in her riding clothes."

"And Tom?"

"Oh, darling, don't be too eager to run into Tom. He and Iris have separate bedrooms. She's, what you'd call, 'frigid.' Tom has a room in the east wing, nowhere near hers."

I'm seriously having trouble reconciling this new information about Iris being frigid with my knowledge of her having an affair with Vassili. Looks like I have more mysteries on my hands than a murder.

"Good to know. Can you show me to Iris's room? Maybe you can keep watch outside so I can make a more thorough search. I don't want to get caught by Iris, but I especially don't want to get busted by the horrible woman that runs the household."

"Mrs. Charles?" Liliané chuckles. "Mrs. Charles is the epitome of efficiency and service. You could learn a great deal from her, darling."

"In another lifetime, perhaps. Unfortunately, she thinks I'm British, and I'm struggling to remember my accent when she comes around. But I already received one warning from her this morning, so if I don't want to be fired on my first day, I can't really afford to get caught again."

"Liliané Barnes does not keep watch."

I kick out my hip and cross my arms. "Then Liliané Barnes is never going to find out who killed her. You want answers? You brush off that snobby façade and put in the work."

She raises her perfectly plucked eyebrows and blinks in shock. "You are a delicious conundrum. Follow me."

Maybe I should hang up a shingle as a ghost therapist? Their afterlife issues definitely seem to be interfering with my sleuthing.

Liliané leads the way to her eldest daughter's quarters.

I step inside and close the door.

She promises to keep an eye out for Mrs. Charles.

The bedroom is in stark contrast to its resident. Iris is prim, proper, and perfectly put together. This room is . . . It's a disaster.

Clothes strewn everywhere, a wet towel on the floor—on the Persian-carpeted floor.

Beauty products spread from one end to the other, across the vanity in the bathroom, and the trash in the waste bin is overflowing.

Curling my lip in disgust, I survey the heap of wastepaper, empty cosmetic bottles, and—

Is that a— Oh boy! I am loving this trash! Oscar the Grouch could not love this trash more than me!

CHAPTER 11

AFTER A HASTY SEARCH through the vanity drawers, I find a plastic bag filled with cotton puffs. I open the bag, dump the cotton balls in the drawer, and proceed to recover my trash treasure.

Turning the bag inside out over my hand, I grab the item from the trash, reverse the bag, roll it up, and tuck it in my apron.

I'm in such a hurry to alert Liliané, I almost forget my feather duster. I spin back toward the bathroom, as the bedroom door bursts open.

"What do you think you're doing in my room?"

Uh oh. It's Iris, and she's not pleased to see me.

When in doubt lie it out. And don't forget you're British. "Sorry, m'arm. The regular maid left her feather duster in 'ere and I was sent to fetch it."

Iris skulks toward me, but before she can get

close enough to question my identity, I scurry back into the bathroom, grab my feather duster, and curtsy twice as I race out of her room.

I'm making a beeline for the servants' stairwell as Iris shouts down the hallway. "Mrs. Charles is going to hear about this!"

As soon as I'm out of sight, I lean up against the wall, with one hand on my chest, and try to catch my breath. "Whew, wow, that was close."

Liliané lazily floats through the doorway. "Oh, there you are, darling. I completely lost track of you."

"You were supposed to be standing guard."

"What? That doesn't sound like me."

"Iris came back and caught me in her room."

"Oh, that is unfortunate, darling. No one is ever supposed to be in her room."

"What? Why didn't you tell me that before I went in?"

"She was out riding. How should I know when she'd be back?"

"That's the purpose of the lookout."

Mrs. Charles storms around the corner. "Whom are you speaking to?"

"Hmmmm?"

"I distinctly heard you speaking to someone."

"Sorry, m'arm. I keep myself to myself."

Mrs. Charles exhales and crosses her arms in

anger. "I warned you that Mr. Barnes is no longer in charge of hiring. Whatever you did to get this job—" she scoffs "—the only way you're going to keep it is by actually cleaning this house." Off she marches down the stairs, in her sensible shoes, without waiting for a reply.

When I'm certain she's out of earshot, I mumble, "Rude."

"Better get to work. Vassili's not here to save your ample behind."

Before responding, I listen carefully for footsteps, and check down the hallway. Even though I don't see anyone, I keep my voice low. "Is there somewhere we can speak uninterrupted?"

Liliané chuckles. "At least a hundred places. Follow me, darling."

I follow her, but the "darling" thing is wearing on my nerves.

She sweeps down the hallway like she owns the place and, by all accounts, she did. My ghost guide floats up a wide staircase to the third floor and through a closed door.

Coming to an abrupt halt on my side, I jiggle the handle and whisper, "It's locked."

Her head pushes through the thick mahogany. "I thought you said you were a sleuth. No sleuth worth her weight in pounds sterling gets by without knowing how to pick a lock." Her face vanishes back through the door like smoke being sucked into a vacuum tube.

I glance up and down the hallway, slide a bobby pin out of my wig, and do my worst.

And, to be sure, it is my worst. It takes me a full minute and a half to gain access to the room.

Once inside, I lock it behind me.

As I've learned, from every mystery television show I've ever watched, the fastest way to get discovered is to leave a door open.

"Now, where's the key to that door?"

She smirks. "Mrs. Charles is the only one with a key." Her laughter grates, like fingernails on a chalkboard.

"Fine. We don't have much time. I have some very important information, but first I need to ask you some questions."

"Fire away, darling. I'm an open book. I've already paid the ultimate price for my art."

And there it is again, a not-so-subtle reference to her Post-Impressionist collection. "Isadora says you're a con artist, or possibly more. Elaborate."

"Certainly. I'm a bit of a con artist, but mostly I'm a small-time art thief."

"Small-time? Cézanne. Rousseau. Van Gogh. Matisse. These are not small-time artists."

Liliané appraises me with a whole new appreciation. "You are much more than you seem. Fair enough. I *was* a small-time art thief, until I met Vassili."

"You acquired all of that artwork in the last three years?"

She clicks her tongue condescendingly. "Hardly. I've been sending *presents* home for over forty years. The first few were honest mistakes. I'd stumble upon a little treasure here or there and offer a modest sum. Eventually, when my offers were refused, I stopped asking."

Sinking onto a red-velvet upholstered chair, I let out a low whistle. "So how does Vassili fit into this?"

"Ah, the lovely Vassili. We actually met about thirteen years ago, both trying to steal the same Picasso. He was younger, faster, and he got what I wanted. I was wealthy and patient, and I got it back. Eventually, we came to an understanding. A woman of my means and maturity could pass through customs much more easily than a handsome, yet suspicious-looking, man such as Vassili. I retired from active collecting, and let him do all the legwork."

"Sounds like the perfect arrangement. So why marry him?"

"Yes, there's the rub. This recent attempt on my life, although successful, wasn't the first. I honestly feared for my safety in my own home, and I knew that if I married Vassili and left everything to him, he would take the artwork and leave the rest to the family. It was the perfect arrangement . . ."

I swallow and shake my head. "Until someone killed Vassili."

"Poor little lamb."

She exhales dramatically and attempts to fling her ghostly form onto the bed. It's, of course, more comical than climactic, and I laugh out loud.

"The folly of youth. I think I've given you more than enough to earn a reward. What did you find in Iris's room?"

I slip my hand in my pocket, pull out the plastic bag, and let it unroll dramatically. I can hear the music swell—in my mind.

Liliané shoots off the bed and zips toward the prize in my hand. "A pregnancy test? Is it positive?"

"That's a yes, and a heck yeah. Your frigid daughter is carrying someone's baby. And I hate to be the one to tell you, but the way I saw her flirting with Vassili on the gambling cruise, I think it might be his."

"Impossible." Liliané swirls around the room. Mumbling, exhaling, balling up her fists, in a good old-fashioned ghost snit.

I lean back in the chair, roll the bag up, and tuck it back into my apron.

Eventually, Liliané runs out of steam and floats

in my direction. "It's impossible, impossible, I tell you."

"Not from what I saw."

She dismisses my statement with a flick of her diamond-laden wrist. "Iris is a colossal flirt. That's how she landed Tom. But I'm ninety-nine point nine percent certain she's still a virgin."

"She's nearly forty!"

Her mother shakes her head and lifts her hands in a "don't ask me" gesture. "I'm telling you, it's a serious psychological problem."

"Well, she's a heck of an actress. But you're forgetting, I have the added benefit of psychic senses. There was some legitimate heat between the two of them. I think she may have played you for the fool." Determined to avoid otherworldly rage, I hunker down in my chair, fully expecting a tirade from Liliané.

Instead she floats slowly toward the ceiling, disapparates, and a gentle voice whispers from the void, "I'm going to have a grandchild."

Now that I have my first real clue, it's definitely time for me to get back to work. I grab my feather duster and head for the locked door.

"How am I going to lock this door behind myself?"

Liliané's pending grandmotherhood must've

softened her edge. "There's a spare key in the middle drawer of my antique vanity, darling."

I shake my head and hurry to the drawer. There are a number of keys in the drawer. "Can you be more specific?"

She floats my way, clearly distracted by the bombshell of her frigid daughter's pregnancy. She glances down at all the keys and chuckles. "I'd forgotten I had so many souvenirs." Her silvery white fingers float above the rows as she mumbles the names of, what I assume are, obscure European cities.

"Which one is for this door?"

I can't seem to break through her fog. Her hand lingers over a brass skeleton key, patinaed with age. "We'll always have Paris."

"Liliané, I'm sorry, but I don't have time to stroll down memory lane. I need the key to *this* door, and I need it right—"

Footsteps out in the hallway make my throat tighten with the fear of discovery.

They hesitate for a moment, but after trying the knob and finding the door locked, they continue down the hall.

"Key. Now."

She finally gestures to a fairly modern key on the far left. "This one."

"If there's any chance you can pull yourself together and go spy on Iris, I would love to know if she notices that some of her trash is missing."

My new ghost boss seems utterly mesmerized by her collection of keys and makes no reply.

There's no time. I've got to get back out there before Mrs. Charles returns.

Let's be clear, even without extrasensory perception, we both know who tried the handle at the door.

I unlock the door, open it a crack, look and listen. Seems like the coast is clear.

Slipping out, I pull the door closed behind me and lock it. The key joins the other items in my rapidly filling apron pocket.

There are a number of statues on this floor that look in need of a good dusting. So, I set to work and, before long, actually forget I'm supposed to be snooping.

Leaning across an antique breakfront to dust an intricately carved frame around a portrait of some long-dead noble, an unwelcome presence slips up behind me and tightens their grip on my hips.

Foster brother Jarrell's training kicks in instinctively.

I spin and crack the feather duster handle to the side of the man's head. My knee connects painfully, more so for him, with his groin.

As he leans forward in agony, I drop the feather

duster, grip his skull with both hands, and smash his face onto my rising knee.

My heart is racing and fear is pumping adrenaline through my body so fast, I feel both vulnerable and invincible.

The man stumbles back, one hand on his crotch and one hand catching the blood dripping from his nose.

Well, this is awkward. My assailant appears to be none other than Thomas Becker.

He spits out his retort as blood streams down his face. "What in heaven's name do you think you're doing, young lady? You'll never work as a housekeeping stewardess again in this town. Scuttle that—in this country!"

Looks like I'm fired. No point in playing nice. But I do think that there will be something lovely about insulting him in my horrible cockney accent. "Oi, ain't nothin' in heaven or hell that makes it all right for you to molest me person. Ya filthy muppet."

Leaving the feather duster in the hallway, I make haste to the servants' staircase. As soon as I'm out of sight, I run like the wind.

Blasting into the changing room, I frighten a couple of unsuspecting gals and grab my clothes from the cubby.

Both of them are shouting warnings about getting fired if I leave in my uniform, and other things I don't care about.

All I want to do is get to my Jeep. I'm almost clear when the voice of Mrs. Charles commands me. "And where do you think you're going?"

Once more for the Queen! "Away from this whorehouse, birdie."

Her astonished gasping is almost worth the unwelcome groping. Not quite, but almost.

I jump into my chariot, toss my clothes into the passenger seat, and spit gravel as I fishtail out of the servants' parking lot.

CHAPTER 12

I CAN'T BELIEVE my luck! Not only did I escape the Barnes residence without any *living* soul discovering my true identity, but I also made it out with the evidence.

As the automatic garage door rolls down behind me, I stride down the alley, bursting with pride. I slip my key in the lock and twist.

SNAP.

Blerg. The door is not open and, bonus, the key snapped off in the lock.

I bang on the door, but neither Grams nor Twiggy comes to my aid.

It's Sunday. Chances are greater than usual that Twiggy's not here. And Grams is likely squirreled away on the third floor of the museum, writing more query letters.

I don't have time to wait for a locksmith, but I'm not a helpless damsel in distress. Several months ago, Silas taught me how to use magic—apologies, Silas—alchemy, to get out of handcuffs.

And, not that long ago, I successfully used the same techniques to open his front gates. I probably could've tried this at the mansion, but fear of discovery would've played havoc with my focus.

Placing my hands over the lock on the alleyway door and breathing calmly, I use the imagery of ice becoming liquid—changing the state from locked to unlocked.

The handle spins and the door opens.

I dance a little victory dance in my maid's uniform in the alley, and, as I'm spinning around, wiggling my hips, I catch sight of the alley door to my father's building.

Hmmmm.

The saying is "pride cometh before the fall," but clearly we're already past the fall and I'm climbing back up the next hill.

Slipping off one of my white trainers, I wedge it in the doorjamb of the bookshop and walk across the alleyway to try my luck on door number two.

Eyes closed. Hands in position. Transmutation of matter.

CLICK.

And just like that, I've opened another one!

Stepping inside, I'm suddenly overcome by the tingling urge to have a little poke around. Sure, I've been here before, but the thrill of sneaking through a big empty building is too tempting to resist. I walk into the lobby, admiring all the details my father recreated in his post-fire redesign. Three lovely stories. Terrazzo floors, ornamental plaster cornices, and marble walls in the elevator lobby.

A quick flash of heebie jeebies races over my skin when I turn and see the life-size statue of my grandfather, Cal Duncan, my grandmother's dearly departed third husband.

Walking over, I look up into his face. With the afternoon sun slanting across the lobby, in the soft warm light, he looks almost human. I drift off into one of my daydreams about what life would've been like growing up as the granddaughter of this wealthy railroad tycoon and living on an actual estate.

The first time I saw Cal's place, I wasn't prepared. From the large granite stone bearing the Duncan family crest, through the massive wrought-iron gates, and down the birch-lined drive. I was immediately struck by the sheer size of the mansion. Perched on the shore of the great lake that graces the entire region, but actually rivaling the body of water in beauty. Breathtaking.

It's a shame it had to be—

"Don't move. Keep your hands where we can see them."

Uh oh. This is going to be awkward. And did he say "we?" Great.

Sheriff Harper approaches, claps one half of his handcuffs around my right wrist, twists the arm behind my back and, as he's locking it around my left wrist, I can no longer resist. "I really don't think my dad's going to press charges."

Erick spins me around, looks me over, head to toe, twice, and is unable to find words.

"I can explain." I tilt my wig-clad head back and forth playfully.

"At ease, Paulsen. It's Moon."

Deputy Paulsen exhales loudly, but does not holster her weapon.

"I can't wait to hear the explanation for all of this." Erick gestures to my outfit as he pulls out his phone. "But first, we're going to call Jacob Duncan and you're going to explain why his silent alarm went off on a Sunday afternoon."

The ringing in the speakerphone stops abruptly. "Everything all right, Sheriff Harper?"

"Good afternoon, Jacob. I believe I'll let your daughter explain."

"Hey, Dad. Funny story."

To my father's credit, he chuckles before I even

tell him the story. "First, tell me you're okay, Mitzy."

"I'm perfectly fine. Silas asked me to check the locks on your alleyway door. Good thing I did. It was . . . unlocked."

To his credit, he keeps his subsequent chuckling under control. "Good man, that Silas. I guess I'm lucky you checked."

"Right?" I nod my superiority at the sheriff.

Erick shakes his head. "Jacob, am I correct in assuming you won't be pressing breaking and entering charges?"

My father exhales. "You are correct, Sheriff."

"Understood. I don't want to leave your building unsecured while you're out of town. Is there someone you can send over to check the system?"

"Absolutely. I'll take care of it right away. I'll be back in town on Tuesday. Mitzy, you go ahead and keep an eye on the place until then."

"No problem, Dad. We'll have dinner when you get back."

Erick taps the speaker button off and puts the phone to his ear. "Sorry to bother you, Mr. Duncan. You have a good trip . . . Not a problem. Doing my job, sir." He slips his phone back in his pocket, crosses his arms in that yummy way that makes his biceps bulge, and stares at me as though he's looking straight through to my soul.

"There's a perfectly good explanation. And I promise it's absolutely worth the wait. Can you give me a chance to head back to the bookshop and cleanup? I'll get changed, and I promise to give you a call."

A scoff in the distance, followed by metal sliding into leather, indicates Deputy Paulsen has heard enough and finally re-holstered her gun.

But if I know her, and unfortunately I do, one hand is still resting on the grip. I'm pretty sure she's one of those people who sleeps with their gun. And I don't mean under her pillow. I mean next to her, possibly on its own pillow.

Erick hasn't replied, and he's still staring at me with a heaping helping of suspicion.

"Sheriff Harper, as much as I enjoyed you putting me in handcuffs, I'm going to need my hands free to, you know, get changed."

"No problem, Moon. Answer one simple question and you'll be out of those cuffs."

"This feels like a trap."

"Interesting word choice. You mind telling me how you got in this building when the alarm was clearly armed?"

Little gears inside my head churn and whir in earnest. "The door was—open."

He uncrosses his arms and sighs. "Are you telling me or asking me? Because that sounded more like a question than an answer."

"It was open. I thought I heard a noise and then —the thing about Silas." Remind me not to log this down as my best lie ever. Come on, get it together, Mitzy. You're better than this.

"Then Deputy Paulsen and I better check the rest of this building for a possible intruder. You go ahead and return to your bookshop. I'll expect a call from you before five."

"Copy that."

He unlocks the handcuffs and I hurry out, as best I can with one shoe. Once clear of the Duncan Restorative Justice Foundation, I rub my wrists. There's a little cloud of guilt floating over me for forcing him to search an entire building, but what options did I have?

Across the alley, I grab my shoe out of the door, pop into my bookshop, and slam the metal door behind me.

All right. Time to call a locksmith, get changed, and bring Grams up to speed.

"Ree-ow." Soft but condescending.

As I crouch to pet my fiendish feline, he dodges my hand and smacks his right paw firmly on my apron.

"Ree-ow."

"Sorry, I should've said it as soon as I came in. Pyewacket is the smartest cat in all of the land. Yes, your furriness, you were right. You and your baby rattle were right."

He seems to lift his chin in an obvious "I told you so," and then he sits back on his haunches and pays special attention to his glorious whiskers.

Time to tempt Sheriff Harper. A text seems to carry the right amount of mystery. "If you bring me a burger and fries from the diner, I'll pay you in information. FYI this information might even warrant a slice of pin cherry pie à la mode."

Surprisingly, Erick texts back almost immediately. "Deal. On both counts."

Now I have three things to look forward to. Four if you count Erick!

"Grams, Grams, are you still in the closet?"

She drifts out, but her normally creaseless features are pinched with concern.

"What's the matter? I thought you wanted to hear all about my day as a maid."

"You're sure? You're sure she said 'We'll always have Paris'?"

"Yes. I'm sorry, but that's what she said."

She frowns and sighs. "Before, all I had were my suspicions. Max was killed in the car accident before he could confess, and I chose to remember him as we were, not for one possible indiscretion."

"I don't think it changes what you and Max had. Liliané is a grade-A manipulator. Whether she had genuine feelings for Max or not, her entire existence is about collecting trophies. I don't think she cares what happens to the people she takes those trophies from."

"All of our decisions brought us to where we are, right?" Grams mumbles and dabs at her ghostly tears with the back of her hand. Her expression begs for confirmation.

Smiling, I offer some consolation. "One day at a time. Your life was filled with happiness, and your afterlife is amazing. Am I right?"

She laughs lightly and swirls toward me. The energetic hum of her hand against my cheek warms my heart. "My afterlife is better than my life ever was."

BING. BONG. BING.

"He's here!" We cry out in unison.

"Is that what you're wearing?"

"Grams, do not start with me. You stay up here in the apartment, and do not, I repeat, do not pop in on my date."

She lifts her chin and widens her eyes. "So you're admitting it's a date? No more of this 'I'm just a CI filing a report' nonsense?"

"Give it a rest, Isadora." I turn and shush her one more time before opening the bookcase door and running down to answer the bell for the heavy metal door that leads to the alleyway.

Erick steps in, scoops me in his arms, and kisses my—cheek.

Boy, this guy knows more about anticipation than Heinz Ketchup! But as soon as I see the takeout from Myrtle's Diner, I don't have time to play kissy face.

We settle into our chairs in the back room, and I dive into my burger.

He grins. "I'm not going to get between you and those fries, but I'm honestly curious what you have."

This is the moment I've been waiting for. I lean back and wipe my mouth with the paper towel/napkin, and reach into my pocket. "Drumroll, please."

To his credit, Erick immediately taps out a two-finger flourish on his side of the table.

I grip the edge of the plastic bag and unfurl my find.

The relaxed humor immediately drains from Erick's face. He's as white as a ghost. And, as you know, I'm kind of an expert in that area.

"Well?"

Beads of sweat are forming at his temples. He

can barely stutter his reply. "You're— But we never — How?"

For a psychic, I can be pretty stupid. But all of the bats have finally flown out of the belfry and the lights are shining at a thousand megawatts. "It's not mine! Dear Lord baby Jesus, it's not mine!"

The wall of tension dissipates. However, the level of discomfort skyrockets.

Erick swallows audibly. "It's not that there's anything wrong with kids. I didn't mean—"

I hastily jump in to throw my pathetic efforts into guiding our vessel back toward calmer waters. "No, of course not. Kids are great. I mean, for some people. I mean, when people are ready, or have a plan, or whatever."

Our widened, fear-dilated eyes meet across the table and, thankfully, we both burst into laughter.

He's the first to recover. "We're a long way from having that discussion, right?"

I nod emphatically. "I'm so sorry. I was so wrapped up in my dramatic reveal . . . I clearly didn't think it through."

A degree of relief settles around us, and whatever weirdness happened will definitely be swept under the carpet and addressed at a much, much later date.

"So we've established it's not yours. Are you going to tell me where you got that—test?"

"Definitely. I should've led with, 'Look what I found in Iris's trash bin, when I was pretending to be a maid at the Barnes estate'."

Erick leans back and laces his fingers behind his head. "So your theory about Iris having an affair with Vassili could be more than a theory. But how do we know it's not the husband's?"

"Obviously we don't know that." It warms my heart to hear him say "we," with regard to the investigation. "However, if it was Tom's baby, I'd expect a woman like Iris to send out engraved announcements and be planning the world's most elaborate gender-reveal party. But it will be easy enough to find out. Now that you have this evidence, you can put Iris on the spot and surprise her with the pregnancy test. I'm sure she's a mess of hormones and she'll crack under the pressure in no time."

"Geez, you're ruthless."

"Not necessarily. I happen to be well versed in television detective-show interrogation techniques. The surprise evidence is a classic." I flash my eyebrows conspiratorially. "Can you bring her in for questioning? Can I observe?"

Erick chuckles and runs a hand through his hair. The blond bangs swing down adorably over one eye, and I smile in spite of my weak attempt at self-control. He sighs. "I need to question each of the family members separately. There's no reason I can't start with Iris."

"All right. Let me know when I'm needed at the station. I've got to call Silas."

He tilts his head and grins. "I know that look. What plan are you hatching?"

I bat my eyes innocently. "Hatching? A plan? Little ol' me?"

He shakes his head in defeat. "Let me know if you find out anything?"

I slide out of my chair, lean dangerously close to Sheriff Too-Hot-To-Handle, and whisper, "As per our agreement, Sheriff."

He makes no reply. Instead, he steals a kiss and sends a shockwave of tingles rocketing down to the tips of my toes.

Abruptly standing, I struggle for air.

He smiles wickedly. "You're not the only one full of surprises, Moon."

CHAPTER 13

WAVING TO ERICK, I watch him drive out of the alley. I can't believe I'm dating a cop! A juvenile delinquent and a sheriff. Go figure.

I pull out my phone and call Silas. "Good evening, Mr. Willoughby. How are you on this fine day?"

Once again, Silas finds my formality amusing and takes his time enjoying a chuckle before he replies to my greeting.

Having dispensed with his mandatory pleasantries, I dive into the true purpose of my call. "I was wondering what would happen if someone discovered that Vassili had a child?"

Silas informs me that there is no record of Vassili fathering any children and repeats the information about the contingent beneficiary clause being activated.

"I understand. But I found something out at the manor that could change all of that."

He agrees to meet me at the bookshop as soon as possible, and I hurry up the circular staircase to my apartment to update the murder wall.

Surprisingly, Grams is already in the apartment, swishing back and forth in front of the rolling board as though it's her investigation to solve.

"Well, I am an integral part of the team, dear."

I simply point to my lips and shake my head.

"Sorry, sweetie."

"Actually, I could use your help. There are a couple things from the night of Vassili's murder that I almost forgot about. If you can work on putting together some torn bits of paper—kind of a ransom-note jigsaw puzzle—I need to sit down and replay my memory of the crime scene. I'm sure there's a detail or two that could help us."

Entering the closet to fetch the torn bits of paper from my 1920s handbag, I let out a small scream.

Grams races into the closet. "What is it? Did you see a mouse?"

"Not exactly." I tilt the open handbag toward her.

She gasps and throws a bejeweled hand over her mouth. "Where did you get that?"

"Dad sort of took it from one of Leticia Whitecloud's bodyguards, the one called Jimmy."

Grams nods, and her opalescent eyes drift off into memory. "I remember Jimmy. He was a real good kid. Great football player—I think. He and your dad were friends in high school. At least until that no-good Darrin pulled your father off course."

I stare into the purse at the handgun and ponder my options. "Obviously, I'm not going to give it back to Jimmy. Do you think I should give it to Erick? It's probably not registered and I'm sure there's no serial number. Maybe I should hang on to it. You know, for protection."

A mischievous sparkle emanates from Ghostma. "Who am I going to tell?"

We share a snicker.

Double-checking that the safety is on, I tuck the handgun into the back of my wig drawer.

Out at the coffee table, I tip the glittering, beaded-handbag upside down and dump out the contents. Scooping the paper shreds into a pile, I point at them. "Violet was trying to toss this overboard when I ran into her. I know all the pieces aren't here, but hopefully you can put enough together for us to figure out what she was trying to get rid of."

Grams zooms through the scalloped-back chair and hovers over the torn bits of paper. "I'm on the case."

I chuckle. "That's my line."

While she busies herself with the paper puzzle, I fluff up a couple pillows and get comfortable in my four-poster bed. Laying my hands on my stomach, I feel my breath going in and out. Closing my eyes, I call up the memory of the casino boat and the night of Vassili's murder.

The damp air hangs on my skin. A hint of diesel fuel wafts up from the engines. My kitten heels click-scrape on the nonskid decking.

As I round the corner to the small observation area at the stern, I search through images of the deck, railing, and surrounding area.

There are several scuff marks on the deck near the port side of the boat, where Vassili's body was —found.

The rope, clearly a weapon of opportunity, is tied securely to the top rail. I zoom into the memory to get a closer look.

It's no ordinary knot. It resembles a hangman's noose, but with only two loops around the main rope and then the end comes back through the loop. That's definitely tied by someone with experience. Possibly a yachtie? A term that I learned from my father. I can't really think of other areas that require knowledge of knots, other than the Boy Scouts, but I don't think Vassili was killed by an errant Boy Scout.

At the very edge of the deck in a tiny depression, where possibly a screw is missing, there's a little black chunk of—

"It's a boarding pass!" Ghost-ma rockets toward the tin-plated ceiling and positively glows with pride.

My concentration is utterly shattered. I guess I'll go check out this pass.

Grams made quick work of what most would've considered trash. The bits that she connected contain a gate number, a seat number, and the last three letters of a city. "Is that 'nos'?"

"I think so, but it's a shame we can't see the rest of the destination, or the date." She crosses her arms and shakes her head in defeat.

I quickly pull out my phone and can barely contain my glee. "I realize this is the town that tech forgot, Grams, but this bit over here"—I point to a larger chunk of the sheet—"this is a QR code. If there's enough left for me to scan with my phone, we'll know a lot more than the date."

Hovering my phone over the scrap of paper, I try to keep from shaking with anticipation. The crosshairs zoom in and lock onto the image, there's a click, and away it goes to a website.

"Is it working? Let me see." Grams slips her translucent head between me and the phone, but strangely I can still see fairly well.

"It's definitely a boarding pass. The departure date was the morning after the memorial cruise. And the destination is—"

"Mykonos, Greece!" Grams shouts excitedly.

"Way to steal my thunder."

She attempts to hide her light under a bushel and seem apologetic.

"So, Violet was planning on going to Greece the morning after her mother's service. The real question is, was she going alone?" I tap my index finger on my bottom lip.

Grams wags a finger at me. "No. I think the real question is, *why* was she going to Greece? What if she knew something about Vassili's past that would have stymied his claim to the inheritance? Maybe she had a plan to keep the money out of his hands."

"Maybe. But even if she found a way to invalidate his claim, the contingent beneficiary clause would still kick in, and the money would go to the shelter and the pet cemetery. Why would she fly all the way to Greece to gather information that wouldn't really help her?"

My cohort floats toward our corkboard of clues, and I pace from the murder wall to the large 6 x 6 windows. "Maybe there's more to it. Maybe she was onto something that would have invalidated the entire will. I'll have to check with Silas—"

BING. BONG. BING.

"It's Silas! Right on cue." I run downstairs and let Silas in. However, my manners fail me and I begin blurting out my evidence willy-nilly. ". . . the boarding pass was for a flight to Mykonos. Did I tell you about the knot? Do you know anything about knots?"

As the bookcase door to my hidden apartment slides open, Silas holds up a hand to stanch the flow of words pouring out of my mouth. "Perhaps, you will allow me the luxury of a seat before I attempt to respond to your multiple queries?"

Sufficiently admonished, I gesture for Silas to make himself comfortable on the overstuffed settee while I pace impatiently in front of the growing wall of 3 x 5 cards.

"The pregnancy test will certainly be of interest. If the child is Mr. Becker's, then the matter would be closed. However, if Iris bears the progeny of Vassili, she would indeed possess a powerful measure to oppose the will's contingency."

"What about that knot? Does it sound special? Like the kind of knot only a certain person could tie?"

"As informative as I found your description,

without seeing the actual knot, I fear I may be of little use."

I shrug. "I could try and draw it. I'm not super artistic or anything, but I could give it a shot."

Silas leans back, smooths his bushy mustache with a thumb and forefinger, and studies me in an unnervingly careful way.

Rolling my eyes, I let my shoulders droop. "I feel a lesson brewing."

He harrumphs and crosses his arms. "Then you should count yourself among the lucky few."

Taking a seat in the scalloped-backed chair, I fold my hands in my lap and await further instructions.

"Although I fear this may be beyond your gifts, we would be remiss if we did not at least make the attempt."

The faint taste of copper spills across my tongue as I literally bite the edge of it to keep myself from interrupting my mentor.

"Call up the image of the knot and send it to me."

And that's the end of my rope, folks. "Send it to you? Like an email? What are you talking about?"

"Do you remember when I taught you to pluck an answer from a subject's consciousness, regardless of whether they were to speak the answer out loud or simply hold it in their mind?"

"Yeah."

He scowls.

"Yes, sir."

"This exercise is similar, but instead of seeking the information within my consciousness, you will take the information from your consciousness and place it in mine. Like a letter, or perhaps an email, if that is easier for you to comprehend."

I sit back in the chair and my stomach swirls with anxiety.

"Close your eyes. Release your fear of failure. And call up the image."

I do as I'm told. The image of the knot on the railing of the *Jewel of the Harbor* snaps into crisp focus.

Somehow sensing my success, he continues the lesson. "Now show me that image, as simply and confidently as if you were handing me a photograph."

I don't have time to tell him that people no longer carry photographs, but instead have hundreds, if not thousands, of electronic images on their smartphones. But I get the analogy. I exhale and return my focus to the image of the knot. Then I try to show it to Silas.

He mumbles something under his breath. "Almost there. Release your hold on it. Give it to me."

Not sure whether I'm releasing the image of my

own free will or if I'm being commanded to do so, I *give* him the knot.

He exhales. "Ah! I see what you mean. It is indeed a unique ligature. A yachtsman could definitely have tied this. To be certain, we need to see the lashing at the other end. Do you believe you hold enough sway over the sheriff to procure a glimpse of the crime scene photos?"

I exhale and open my eyes. "I probably hold enough sway, but I don't want to see photos of what's at the other end of that rope. You ask him. You look at it and let me know."

Silas chuckles. "Fair enough. I will endeavor to acquire that access. Are you able to return to your employment at the manor tomorrow?"

"Um, that's a big 'not on your life.' I gave Mr. Becker a bloody nose today."

It's not often that I catch Silas completely off guard. But his jowls and the corners of his mustache both rise in shock. "Will he be pressing charges?"

I laugh heartily. "Highly unlikely, since the bloody nose was a direct result of him sexually harassing me in the hallway."

Silas tilts his head and smooths his mustache. "Any witnesses?"

"None living. I'd say there's a greater than fifty percent chance that Liliané's ghost saw what happened."

Silas nods, as though discussing whether or not the eyewitness statements of ghosts are admissible in court is an everyday occurrence. "I suspect you're right. I doubt Mr. Becker will pursue the matter. However, it is in your best interest not to return to the manor."

I flash him a thumbs up. "We're on the same page."

Grams floats through our discussion and Silas shivers with ghost chills. "Isadora, is that you?" He reaches into the pocket of his tattered tweed coat and removes his wire-rimmed spectacles. He hooks the curved arms over his large ears and the rose-hued lenses warp the curvature of his eyes. "Ah, there you are. What do you make of this pregnancy test?"

"Well, I only had the one child, as you know, and it was carefully planned with Cal. But Liliané used all three of her pregnancies to trap her unsuspecting suitors. There's a chance that Iris is simply using the baby to get her hands on Vassili's money. It's a very 'Barnes' thing to do." She scoffs angrily.

I'm not sure why she's so offended by the actions of this family, but I nod my agreement.

Silas leans forward and gestures toward the specter of my grandmother. "Would you be so kind, Mizithra?"

"Oh, right." Apparently, I'm ignoring my other-world-interpreter duties. I quickly fill Silas in on Grams' honey-pot theory, and he agrees, with some reservation.

"That is one possible explanation. I fear we won't be able to put the pieces in the correct order until we obtain the last one."

"I need to see what else I can retrieve from my mental images of the crime scene. Will you follow up with Erick?"

"Indeed. However, in the interest of protecting your special relationship with our local sheriff, it would behoove you to share the rest of your information with him before I request a favor."

"That's what I like about you, Silas. You're always thinkin'. Always got my best interests at heart."

Both he and Grams laugh a little too easily.

Silas regains his composure and rises from the settee. "Perhaps if you repeat that enough times, you will come to accept its truth."

Without another word, he presses the ornate plaster medallion that activates the secret door and quietly takes his leave.

Grabbing my phone, I take a picture of the partially reassembled boarding pass and text it to Erick, with the message, "Hope it's not too late. I rescued these from the deck of the casino boat. Violet was attempting to toss them overboard. Any update on when you'll be questioning Iris?"

He replies with an eye roll emoji and the requested update. "She's coming in of her own free will . . . first thing in the morning. If you bring in the evidence, you can wait in my office."

"You've got a deal, Sheriff."

I enjoy the shorthand we're developing. He says "office" and I know he means observation room. It definitely feels like progress to be working with him on solving the case, rather than solving cases in spite of him.

"Are you going down to the station, dear?"

"Since you already know the answer to that question, thought-dropper, I'm going to go ahead and ignore it. Can you add our new information to the board?"

Grams attempts to stand at attention in her designer gown and pops a bejeweled salute.

Despite the effort at serious discipline, I continue laughing all the way to bed.

I remove the chain from around my neck and hold the hefty, cool brass key in my hand.

Laying it on my bedside table, I drift off, tingling with the memory of Erick's stolen kiss.

CHAPTER 14

MY ONE-OF-A-KIND, triangle-barreled, designer key slips easily into the well-disguised lock in the front door. Twisting the key three times, I secure the door and let my fingers drift over the intricate carving for a moment before turning to walk down to the sheriff's station.

My favorite deputy, Furious Monkeys, actually looks up and smiles when I walk in.

I tilt my head and scrunch my nose in confusion. "Did you lose your phone?"

She laughs nervously. "No, thank goodness. My battery died, and it takes a few minutes to charge back up before the screen comes on."

Nodding, I smile. "That makes more sense. What level are you now?"

"I cracked 200 this morning."

"Wow."

She waves me through the crooked, swinging wooden gate toward Erick's office and I don't hesitate to accept the invitation.

Unfortunately, Deputy Paulsen is in the bullpen. She's leaned back precariously on her wooden rolling chair and has her spit-shined boots kicked up on top of her metal desk.

I hope that if I don't make eye contact I can pass by unseen.

"Hey, Moon?"

No such luck.

"Good morning, Paulsen."

"I can't imagine what a spoiled little rich kid like you would be doing working as a maid. What were you up to in the outfit, eh?"

Now, I'm going to warn you that this is an inappropriate response, but this woman knows exactly how to push my buttons. I step toward her desk, lean down, and lower my voice. "You know, just between us girls, I don't think Erick would appreciate me talking about what goes on behind closed doors, but you know how some men feel about maids' uniforms."

Her snarky, gum-chewing jaw clamps to a halt, and my extrasensory perceptions pick up on a rapid increase in her heartbeat.

There is no way I'm gonna blow that exit line,

so I spin and march into Erick's office before she can think of a comeback.

"Hey, Mitzy, I wasn't sure you'd make it in."

I smile. "Sorry, I'm all out of snappy comebacks. I used my best one on Paulsen, thirty seconds ago."

He shakes his head. "Go easy on her. I know she's a little much, but she's a good cop."

"If you say so." I hand him the bag containing the pregnancy test, and fish the torn pieces of the boarding pass out of my pocket.

He exhales loudly. "I hope I don't have to answer any chain of custody questions about this stuff. It definitely isn't admissible, but it could help us get a court order, if the need arises." He reaches into his desk drawer and retrieves two actual evidence bags. Carefully sliding the plastic pregnancy test wand from my makeshift bag into his official one, he uses a gloved hand to transfer the torn bits of paper into the other. Making some notations on the bags, he leans back in his chair. "Is there anything else you wanted to tell me about your brief employment at the Barnes mansion?"

I shake my head innocently. "Nope."

"Did you happen to bump into Mr. Becker while you were 'on the job'?"

I swallow audibly and shrug noncommittally. I'm not about to tell him how my knee *bumped* into Tom's unwelcome nose.

Erick shakes his head and exhales loudly. "Yeah, he wasn't real forthcoming about his injuries. I thought you might have a hunch."

Before I'm forced to perjure myself, Paulsen interrupts. "You want the daughter in Interrogation Room One, Sheriff?"

"Yes, Deputy."

I look away from the door and busily pick at a thread on the seam of my jeans while Paulsen takes Iris into the interrogation room. Interestingly, she doesn't return to the bullpen.

"Did Iris come without an attorney?"

"We told her it was a general statement. She's not being charged with anything at this time."

While Erick walks in to conduct the interview with Iris, I slip into the observation room sandwiched between the station's two interrogation spaces.

Flipping the silver switch above the speaker, I train my eyes and my psychic senses on Iris.

Erick clearly hasn't watched as many detective shows as me. After he gets the particulars from Iris, he jumps right to the pregnancy test. No buildup. No suspense. No gotcha.

My extra senses tingle in anticipation of her answer and I lean forward.

Iris slowly straightens in her chair and her gaze seems to pierce through the one-way glass. Her hands fall to her lap, and her right hand rises slowly toward her chin, as though she's zipping up an invisible zipper.

Even though I'm positive she can't see me, the target-lock of her eyes is unnerving. And as quickly as I thought I was picking up a possible clairsentient message, it feels as though a door slams in my face.

Iris crosses her arms and leans back in her chair.

I'm getting nothing. No messages. No visions. No idea what she's feeling.

Her sharp angular jaw grinds once before she tilts her beak-like nose upward. "Any woman would know that's obviously a pregnancy test stick, Sheriff. However, if you have a specific question for me, please ask."

Erick may be kind and honest, but he's no fool. "Mrs. Barnes-Becker, one of your employees turned this in to the station. It was recovered from a trash receptacle in your private bathroom. Can you explain how it might have gotten there?"

Iris adjusts her crossed arms and the points of her elbows appear sharp enough to slice paper. "Again, Sheriff Harper, you'll have to ask me a specific question. If you would like me to explain to you how one uses such a test, I'm happy to do so. But if you wish for me to speculate on the activities of my many employees' trash disposal habits, I'm afraid I'm unable to do so."

I pace in a small circle inside the observation room. She's impenetrable. I have to talk to Silas. She did something. She sensed me, and she closed herself off.

Erick sets the bag with the pregnancy test on a stack of papers. His back is to me, but I can sense him giving her a superficial, but polite smile. "Very well. We will be submitting this to the lab and once we have the DNA results, we'll compare them to the samples we have on file from the incident at the estate last year. We may need to question you further."

There's a smug flash in her eyes. "I look forward to it, Sheriff."

He slips another evidence bag to the middle of the table and taps it with his left hand. "Any idea what your sister was planning on doing in Mykonos?"

This information catches Iris off guard. Not that I'm getting any extrasensory information. I have to rely on my years of observing people when I worked in the service industry. You learn to recognize little things, respond accordingly, and hopefully increase your chances of a bigger tip. But her shock could be simply that Erick got his hands on these fragments of the boarding pass, rather than shock about Violet's trip.

She uncrosses her wiry arms and lets her hands

fall to her lap. "Much like the rest of my family, my sister and I are not close. She doesn't feel the need to have her travel plans approved by me."

Erick leaves the bag in the middle of the table, but leans back. "Fair enough. Have you observed anything in the last couple of days that would give you an indication why she canceled her trip?"

Iris twists her head on her thin neck and swallows slowly. "I'm sorry, Sheriff, I've had a lot to deal with recently. My mother passed away, my stepfather was murdered, and I've been disinherited. I'm sure you'll excuse me if I haven't had time to notice the desperate and narcissistic activities of my younger sister."

He slips that evidence bag into a folder, and I get the sense that he's about to end the interview.

Paulsen stands abruptly and pounds her fist on the table. "You're not gonna get away with this."

Iris remains calmly seated, and I wring my hands in frustration. All I wanted was a little peek into her behind-the-scenes.

She exhales her boredom. "Sheriff Harper, am I free to go?"

Erick nods. "Of course, Mrs. Barnes-Becker. We appreciate you coming in today. I'll let you know about the lab results and whether or not we need to schedule a follow-up interview."

Iris stands in one fluid, snake-like move. She

smooths her pencil skirt over her bony hips, and I notice the way her skeletal collarbones protrude as she effortlessly retrieves her large bag from the floor. She gives a curt nod, offers a "Good day," and slithers out of the interrogation room.

I flick the switch off and wait a beat to be sure that Iris is through the bullpen before I open the door to hurry back into Erick's office— And run directly into the waiting Iris.

"Mitzy Moon. I see the rumors are true. Obviously you inherited more than your grandmother's money." She spins on her impossibly high designer heels and struts out of the sheriff's station as though she hasn't a care in the world.

The handle on the interrogation room door twists, and I lunge into Erick's office.

Paulsen slides me a suspicious side-eye as she returns to her desk, and Erick immediately closes his office door behind him when he walks in.

Without waiting for an invitation, I volunteer my opinion. "Well, it doesn't seem like she came down here to be cooperative."

He shrugs. "It's a pretty classic maneuver. She comes down without an attorney, doesn't really tell us anything, but believes she's shrouded herself in the appearance of innocence because she agreed to come alone."

"She's not innocent. She's lying."

He shakes his head. "I know you and your hunches have a pretty good track record, but try to remember how many criminals I've interrogated. There was nothing in her mannerism or word choice to indicate she was lying. We need hard evidence. And if we can't find that, I'll take an eyewitness or a confession any day of the week."

Standing, I shake my head. "She's up to something. And I'm going to figure out exactly what it is." I put a hand on the doorknob.

Erick grips my other arm. "Don't go back to the manor. No matter what they say, one of them is a murderer."

Tilting my head, I have to ask, "Are you taking Leticia and her *muscle* off the suspect list?"

"Not officially but, between you and me, I don't see her being that careless. Vassili owed her a lot of money. She's a smart, patient woman. She wouldn't kill the golden goose right before he got all the gold."

I chuckle. "Good point. See ya 'round, Sheriff."

He sighs. "See ya 'round, Moon."

CHAPTER 15

OUTSIDE THE LOCAL sheriff's station, the weather has taken a dark turn. Ominous clouds and *Wizard of Oz* style winds whipping across the lake have replaced the blue sky and warm sun. I wrap my arms around myself, lower my head, and run for the bookshop.

At the exact moment I cross First Avenue, the heavens open and surprisingly chilly rain beats down on my head. I hurry inside the dry safety of the Bell, Book & Candle, and run straight up to the third floor of the printing museum.

Luckily, I guessed correctly, and Grams is busy scratching out another set of query letters. Glancing over or, rather, through her shoulder, I see that she's signing all of the letters "Mizithra Moon, on behalf of Isadora Duncan." "So you're adding forgery to your list of crimes?"

She drops her pen and vanishes.

I cross my arms and chuckle. "I'd say that's a first. The human actually scares the ghost."

She materializes in front of me, looking paler than usual, but laughing along with me. "I do suppose I deserved that, dear. Heaven knows, I caused you plenty of bladder startles when you first arrived."

Shaking my head, I refuse to remember the sheer number of times she popped out of thin air and scared the bejeezus out of me. But thankfully she's gotten in the habit of using the slow sparkly reentry that gives me enough warning to keep my heartbeat in a natural rhythm. "I've got to call Silas. I'll put it on speakerphone so you can hear too."

She nods and hovers over my left shoulder as I place the call. The voice that answers sounds more than a little sleepy.

"Did I wake you, Silas? If so, sorry about that."

"As a matter of fact, I believe the works of Pliny the Elder no longer hold the fascination they once did. I regret to inform that I have deposited a bit of drool on an otherwise pristine manuscript."

Grams and I share an eye roll. "Fair warning, Grams is listening in. I didn't want to have to repeat my story."

"Very well. Proceed."

"Erick brought Iris in for questioning, and I happened to be eavesdropping in the observation room. When I attempted to use my powers to get some additional information, she seemed to look right through the mirrored glass at me. Then she made this weird zipper-y motion with her hand and shut me out. It was truly bizarre. I couldn't get a single psychic message."

Silas harrumphs. "Perhaps I should have informed you, but I felt it was a family matter. Isadora, if you are indeed listening, I believe you owe your granddaughter an explanation."

Grams attempts to look more like the friendly ghost, Casper, than a Japanese yōkai, but she's not fooling anyone.

"Myrtle Isadora Johnson Linder Duncan Willamet Rogers, what aren't you telling me?"

"Well, I never knew for sure."

I translate for Silas.

"Isadora, come now. You always had your suspicions. In fact, I distinctly remember you relaying that one of the reasons you forbade Jacob from having any contact with Iris was that you feared she would ferret out some of your secrets and report them to Liliané."

"Oh, all right. I did have a little suspicion."

"She's admitting her deception, Silas, but will somebody please fill me in?"

Silas once again harrumphs. "I will be en route posthaste. In the meantime, perhaps your grand-mother will pay heed to her conscience. If not, I will fill in the details when I arrive."

I end the call, cross my arms, and engage in a staring contest with a spirit.

Eventually, Grams throws her glimmering arms into the air. "Fine! Liliané was Cal's second wife."

Ghost-ma ignores my dramatic gasp and continues.

"She used her pregnancy to trap him and they were married less than two years. The divorce was messy, but at least Cal had the foresight to force her to sign a prenuptial agreement. If his attentions hadn't wandered to younger and bustier quarry, I'm sure Lillian would've gotten her claws in deeper and convinced Cal to nullify the prenup! As it was, she left with a small fortune and the daughter who bore her last name, as do all her children. Which, honestly makes perfect sense for a woman who runs around having babies as a means of expanding her empire."

Wagging my finger at Grams, I have to mention, "Careful *Mrs. Kettle*. I dare say a woman with five ex-husbands and a piece of each of their fortunes to show for her efforts can hardly point the finger at Liliané's *pot*."

The ghostly fury of indignation that flares in my grandmother's eyes sends a tingle of fright down my spine.

I hastily throw water on the sparks. "But this is your story. Please continue." Boy, oh boy, I can hardly wait to tell Silas how she's defending herself to the death, and beyond.

"So, I always fancied myself as the source of the psychic gifts in the family, and I was frankly surprised when your father displayed no talents. But it would appear that Cal perhaps had his own secret extrasensory chromosomes, and Iris has always had a little claircognizance. She seems to know things. As near as I can tell she has nothing close to your talent—just the one gift, no more. But it sounds as though she's had some training, and she's definitely learned how to close herself off. You won't get anywhere with that one."

I wave my arms in frustration. "But that's my whole thing. If I can't get the additional information, how do I figure out if she's guilty?"

Grams seems to be channeling Silas when she retorts, "You could always resort to good old-fashioned detective work, like the highly skilled Sheriff Harper. However, I'm sure you're looking for something with a little more flair."

"Rude." I cross my arms and have a little pout of my own.

She swirls closer. "When Silas gets here you can beg him to teach you how to do the dimmer switch thing."

We both look around in silence, waiting for a response that will never come, because, of course, Silas is still en route.

"I'll find that little book he's always referencing and make some coffee." Pausing in the doorway, I add, "Do we have any cookies?"

Ghost-ma raises an eyebrow in disbelief. "You're asking the ghost about the contents of your pantry? Honestly, dear, Pye probably has more knowledge about that than either of us."

"Touché."

As I wander around the Rare Books Loft, it takes longer than anticipated to locate the small tome with the blood-red leather cover. When I finally discover it tucked on a bottom shelf, I place it on the coffee table in the apartment and hurry downstairs as the bookcase slides closed.

First things first, I get a pot of coffee brewing while I rifle through the cupboards in the back room.

"Ah ha!" There's no applause. I carefully un-wrap the packet of mostly unbroken graham crackers and arrange them in a sad little fan on a saucer.

My experience as a server comes in quite handy. I hook my pinky through the handles of two mugs, grip the plate with a thumb and forefinger, and scoop up the coffeepot in my other hand.

I'm exceedingly pleased with myself until I arrive at the candle handle. Lucky for me, the perfect timing of my mentor saves the day. "Silas! Can you get the door for me?"

He opens the sliding bookcase door and peruses my offerings. "I don't recall any mention of refreshments. What do you require?"

There's no point playing dumb with a wizard-y alchemist. "The dimmer thing? Grams said you could teach me how to use it with my powers."

Silas adjusts himself in his favorite scalloped-back chair before he replies. "Ah, yes. You have a tendency toward an aggressive use of your gifts. It may behoove you to understand the subtler side of extrasensory perception. Today, in the observation room, it would appear that you pushed your gifts toward Iris in an attempt to take the answers you wanted. If you were to practice a more balanced approach, you could open yourself to receive information, without alerting her to your efforts."

"Like a stealth fighter?"

"I'll take your word." His tone is more than a little condescending.

"Do you mean that if I disguise my efforts, then she won't feel it? Is that what you're saying?"

"In a manner of speaking. Are you prepared for a lesson?"

"Teach me, Obi-Wan."

He chuckles. In spite of his general lack of pop culture knowledge, he seems to be well versed in the Star Wars mythos.

"Sit quietly, and I will tell you a story. Some parts of the story may be true and some may be false. At the end of the story you will share your findings. If at any time I feel you reaching toward me or prodding at me, you will feel a sharp pinprick in the palm of your left hand. Understood?"

"I guess so. How sharp of a pinprick?"

"Sharp enough."

Silas begins his tale and everything starts out fine. I'm sitting calmly, opening myself up to receive messages, and breathing patiently. But about three minutes into the story, my mind starts to wander and my patience wavers. And I unconsciously reach for the information I want.

A very sharp, very stabby pain hits my left palm and I squeal involuntarily. "*Spartacus!*" I rub my hand and shake it until the pain subsides. "All right,

I get it. But wait, are you psychic? How do you feel me trying to get information?"

"As we have discussed on a plethora of previous occasions, I am an alchemist. I deal with the transmutation of matter. And my studies have delved into a great deal of energetic research, so perhaps I am more aware of what is mine and what is not mine than a great many people. Shall we proceed?"

I manage to grumble my agreement, and he continues with his story.

At the conclusion we review the *facts* of the story and the information I gathered. I am eight for ten on correct interpretations, which isn't bad for my first try at being patient and allowing, versus impatient and snoopy. This whole life lesson/maturity thing better be all it's cracked up to be.

"Thanks, Silas. It was a painful lesson, but I'm pretty sure I'll be able to read Iris next time I get a chance. Speaking of which, can you get me into the Barnes mansion one more time?"

"Because your employment as a housekeeping stewardess met with unexpected termination?"

"You're familiar with the story . . . Wait, what do you mean by housekeeping stewardess? Mr. Becker used that same term."

"Ah, it is a yachtsman's term for a maid. Mr. Becker was employed as a yachtie when he met Iris Barnes. Now he owns a luxury yacht as well as two sailboats. One moored here in our very own great lake, and the other in a marina in the South Pacific. He is an avid seaman."

I'm utterly incapable of stopping my adolescent snickering.

"You'll find it is the appropriate term for those who sail the seas."

"I would never question your vocabulary. I apologize for my inappropriate laughter."

"I have a meeting at the Barnes—"

"Hey! The knot I described on the railing. Is that a knot that Tom would know how to tie?"

A low grumble escapes from his jowls, and I know Silas is displeased with my interruption.

"Sorry for the interruption. It popped into my head all of a sudden."

"Very well. The knot you described could be a double bowline, which would indeed be used by a sailor. However, I will withhold my judgment until I see the photo of the knot at the other end of that line."

"Fair enough. You were saying something about an appointment, before I rudely interrupted. Please continue."

"I have a meeting tomorrow at the mansion, with Iris, to discuss her caretaker duties. I believe it would be appropriate for my assistant to attend."

"Copy that. Dora Donaldson on the job."

Silas chuckles.

"See you in the morning, Mr. Willoughby."

"You and your grandmother have a lovely afternoon. Good day." He pauses, collects several graham crackers from my array, and exits without another word.

As soon as he leaves, I turn accusingly toward Ghost-ma. "Are there any other *half* relatives I need to know about?"

She avoids my question. "You said yourself what a terrible person Liliané is. Why would you have wanted to know about Iris?"

"For one thing, it might have prevented me from tipping my hand at the interrogation, but the biggest reason—honesty."

"I'm sorry, dear. You're right. I should've told you about Iris. And to answer your question, Jacob doesn't have any other partial siblings—which I know of. Cal had a few dalliances before we married, but, as near as I can tell, none of them bore fruit."

"Ewww."

"What? What did I say?"

"Please say 'kids' or 'offspring.' The imagery of 'bearing fruit' is too icky. Thank you kindly."

She ghost snorts, and a little ectoplasm comes out of her nose. "Boy, for a modern woman you sure have a lot of hang-ups, sweetie."

"Whatever. At least I know how to download an app!"

Grams dive bombs me. "Why you little . . ."

I run, screaming with fake fright. "Hussy!"

She chuckles. "Harlot!"

"Loose woman!" I shout over my shoulder.

She zips in front of me and manages to take enough corporeal form to make it feel like I'm trapped in gelatin. "Trollop!"

"Let me go you— you— skank!"

She swirls around me and my skin ripples with goosebumps.

Grams dematerializes.

I fall absolutely still. "How did you do that? I've never gotten goosies around you before . . ."

Isadora slowly fades into view. "Well, the truth hurts, I suppose. I think I actually got a little defensive, maybe even angry. Sorry, sweetie."

I rub my arms vigorously. "Well, don't ever do it again. It was terrifying."

She crosses a bejeweled hand over her bosom. "Cross my heart and hope to—"

Our eyes meet and we both crack up.

"I've got to get everything organized for tomorrow. Truce?"

"Truce."

CHAPTER 16

TUCKING THE LAST BIT of my snow-white hair under the mousy-brown wig, I secure it with a couple of bobby pins and smile at my reflection. "Good morning, Dora Donaldson."

A phantom voice drifts in from the closet. "You'll have to wear the same suit as last time. I don't have anything else that bland."

"Thank you so much for that unnecessary comment, Grams. But I do appreciate you wrangling my wardrobe. Do you remember where we put those prop glasses?"

"Here they are." She bursts through the wall, sans glasses, holding an empty hand toward me.

We exchange a shocked glance and both start giggling. "I guess the glasses have to go around and use the door like a normal human."

She shakes her head. "I keep forgetting I'm a ghost."

I straighten my low ponytail and practice my demure facial expression a couple of times, before heading into the closet to get dressed and put on my glasses.

By the time the doorbell rings, I've managed to down a cup and a half of coffee and two stale apple fritter donuts. Of course, I was forced to endure desperate glowering from Pyewacket until I poured his rations.

As I reach for the door handle, there's a familiar crash in the stacks.

"Do you mind coming in for a minute, Silas? Pyewacket knocked something off the shelf and I'd like to take a quick peek before we leave."

"Certainly."

I dart in between the rows of books until I find the discarded tome. "It's a very old copy of the Boy Scout Handbook," I shout to Silas. "Any ideas?"

"Not at this time, but I suggest we keep the clue at hand."

"Copy that." Suddenly remembering I am supposed to be a demure assistant with a soft, whispery voice and a hint of a lisp, I take another stab at my reply. "Whatever you say, Mr. Willoughby."

He chuckles, and his jowls waggle as his face reddens.

On the way out to the Barnes estate, we discuss our strategy for keeping my identity hidden, while allowing me another snoop.

Upon arriving at the home, we're forced to improvise, due to a sudden and chaotic uprising amongst the staff.

I keep my head low and my lips zipped as we follow Mrs. Charles to the library. On the way, she fills Silas in on the recent debacle.

"Well, I'm telling you, Mr. Willoughby, it is pure scandal. That British trollop was here for one day and managed to assault Mr. Becker and ransack poor Miss Iris's room. The thought!"

To his credit Silas maintains his stoic expression. "So sorry to learn of your troubles, Mrs. Charles. Are you sure Iris is up to this meeting?"

"As you know—" Mrs. Charles closes her eyes briefly and sighs "—she's always been the strongest of the three. She's determined to make the best of these mounting catastrophes. Bless her heart."

I stifle a cough, as I wonder if Iris indeed even has a heart.

Shortly after we take our seats in the library, Silas performs the only part of our pre-rehearsed plan that survived. "Oh, dear me, I seem to have left my briefcase in the car. Ms. Donaldson, would you be so kind as to retrieve it?"

I prepare to reply, soften my voice and lean into the lisp. "Yes, of course, Mr. Willoughby."

Scurrying out of the room, I pull the door closed behind me so that Iris won't see my true trajectory.

I hurry into the Cerulean Bath and whisper-shout for the resident ghost. "Liliané? Liliané, I need to speak to you urgently."

The ever-bored socialite drifts through the door and hovers lazily over the enormous glass bathtub. "I can't believe you actually came back! You never cease to impress. Now, if you can find a way to get me a dry martini with two olives, I'll see that there's a special place in heaven for you, darling."

"We both know you're not headed for heaven, Liliané." I raise an eyebrow and dare her to disagree.

She floats toward the ceiling, but makes no reply.

"Let me get to the point. I'm on the clock."

"Why of course. Far be it from me to slow the wheels of blue-collared progress, darling."

"When were you planning on telling me that Iris is my half aunt?"

"Oh, you are a sly thing. Cal Duncan. The one that got away . . ."

"I'd hardly say he got away. The way Isadora tells it, you got knocked up and trapped him into a very profitable two-year marriage."

Liliané laughs brazenly. "Ah, I'd forgotten you had access straight to the horse's a—"

"I think the phrase you're searching for is 'horse's mouth'."

"Is it?" She admires one of her many diamond pendants and squeaks. "The eighteenth-century emerald pin Massimo gave me after he cheated on me with his tennis coach is missing! Someone robbed me!"

"I think you mean someone robbed your corpse. It must've been taken during the viewing. I remember seeing the two strange holes in your lapel." I point to her suit, where the missing jewelry must've been affixed. "Have you seen it around the house?"

"Silly girl, I only discovered it had been stolen two seconds ago."

For the life of me, I can't seem to remember why I'm helping this self-absorbed tyrant. Time for another line of questioning. "Have you been eavesdropping, as I suggested? I need to know if you've heard anything strange."

"Well, I heard Tom swear a blue streak after a certain British maid vanished on Sunday." Her laughter starts out as the tinkling of bells, but rapidly shifts to a much less pleasant sound. I'd have to say it's reminiscent of a steel fork scraping along glass.

Crossing my arms defensively, I retort, "He deserved everything he got."

"Brava! Brava! He's deserved much worse and gotten far less. However, your actions have created a bit of a conundrum for dear old Mrs. Charles. The rest of the servants are attempting a coup. She's always believed the very best about the family, despite mountains of evidence to the contrary. I suppose ignorance is bliss."

"What about Violet? What has she been up to?"

"Oh, please. My plain, shrinking Violet. I haven't noticed her about. She's probably slipped off on one of her expeditions."

"Slipped off? She's a suspect in a murder case. She's not allowed to leave town."

"You'll have to take it up with her when she returns, darling. What was I to do? A little frost on a mirror or a cold chill in the room? It's hardly enough to keep one a prisoner."

"Great, a third of our suspects are missing."

"I hate to be the bearer of bad news, and please don't kill the messenger— Ha! I made a little joke." She flourishes her hand. "But, I'm afraid you're at least two-thirds short of a suspect list."

"What do you mean?"

"My dear, sweet boy disappeared a few hours after shrinking Violet took leave of the family."

Pacing across the marble tile in the luxurious

bathroom brings no immediate solution to mind. "Well, I have to get Mr. Willoughby's briefcase to complete this ruse. Not sure I'll be returning to this house, but I'm close to figuring out who killed you. Have you remembered anything else? The smallest thing could really help."

"I'm not sure if it's a memory so much as something one assumes, but even in my weakened state, I'm sure I would've struggled. After all, I was hardly ready to die. I was having such fun rubbing my marriage to the gorgeous Vassili in everyone's face. I could've easily evaded death, on that alone, for another year."

Attempting to disregard her vengeful, narcissistic tendencies, I'm forced to agree with one part of her revelation. "I'm sure you did struggle. You may have even scratched your attacker. But if your personal doctor ruled it a natural death, and the medical examiner didn't do an autopsy . . . Great stuff, Liliané. Take care."

As I hurry out the door, I hear the closest thing to a compliment that has probably ever passed through Liliané Barnes' lips—dead or alive. "I'm going to miss that feisty, little fireball."

Racing full speed to Silas's car, I grab the briefcase and hustle back up to the library.

"Did you lose your way, Ms. Donaldson?" The

sharp criticism from Iris raises my hackles, but I refuse to take the bait.

I'm an assistant with a tiny speech impediment. "So sorry, Mr. Willoughby."

"All's well that ends well. Please take your seat."

I sit and stare aimlessly at my hands, while silently repeating over and over, *I will not reach for information. I will let it come to me. I will not reach for information. I will let it come to me.*

Silas opens his briefcase and hands Iris a small stack of contracts. "Please review these documents and have the signatures witnessed by the notary. These clearly explain your duties, the rights and privileges of the charities you'll serve, and your monthly stipend."

"I sincerely appreciate you seeing to this arrangement, Mr. Willoughby."

Her words are all sugar and spice, but my calm, patient psychic catcher's mitt is getting a whole heap of resentment flecked with vengeance. Before my overeager senses can do anything I'll regret, I return to reciting my mantra.

Silas makes his planned enquiry. "I was hoping to see your sister Violet today. Is she unwell?"

Iris scoffs and exhales her disgust. "Violet is always unwell. Poor, weak little V. Always needing extra attention, always needing Mommy to take care of her. Well, with Mommy well and truly gone, apparently, Violet has had an episode and run off to her fortress in the forest."

"How odd." Silas shakes his head slowly. "I wouldn't think a weak, sickly girl like her would have any interest in the forest."

Iris shakes her head and attempts a partial eye roll. "Before she discovered playing the weakling would give her the most attention, she made quite a foray into the land of the tomboy. Did you know she was the first girl to force her way into the Birch County Boy Scouts?"

I nearly lose my grip on my calm center. And, as though Silas feels me slipping, he knocks his briefcase onto the floor to draw attention away from me.

"I beg your pardon, Iris. How clumsy of me. I fear my days of working full-time are coming to an end. I may soon have to forgo my efforts with the local charities and embrace retirement to its fullest."

A mixture of glee and panic washes over her. "Surely you won't retire before we've completed our agreement?"

I hurry to pick up his papers and right his briefcase, while Silas calms her nerves. "Of course not. We'll get this entire arrangement nicely secured and make sure that you and Mr. Becker are well looked after."

Her smug grin oozes victory.

I close his briefcase and wait by the door.

"I'm afraid we must take our leave. I appreciate your time today, and, once again, I am sorry for your loss."

Violet? Boy Scouts? The cold jolt of fear that spikes through my mood ring and forms an icy circle on my left hand takes me by surprise. I'm forced to open the door and leave without my employer's permission, or risk exposure.

Silas makes excuses and follows me through the Passageway of the Masters, down the wide, carpeted stairway, and across the marble entrance. However, he waits until we are clear of the Barnes estate and well down the road before he addresses the situation with Violet.

"It would appear Robin Pyewacket Goodfellow is once again a step ahead."

Nodding my agreement, I chime in. "If Violet found out that Iris was having an affair with Vassili, and has a Boy Scout's experience with knots—she might be our prime suspect."

"Well said. However, this brings us no closer to solving Liliané's murder."

"Actually, I have an idea for that too."

Silas chuckles. "Of course you do."

"Will you see if you can get Erick to meet you

for lunch with the crime scene photos, and I'll pop in to share my idea. What do you think?"

"Aside from the fact that I'm none too eager to peruse photos of Vassili's last moments over my liver and onions, I'm afraid I must agree. Am I dropping you at the bookstore?"

"Yes, please. I'll walk over to the diner in about twenty minutes."

"We have an accord."

Finding myself with no time to change out of my Dora wardrobe and shower away my matted-down, under-wig hair, I opt to stay in character. If nothing else, it will give Erick a laugh and perhaps put him in a more agreeable mood.

"Pyewacket, come and receive your praise and adulation."

And, once again, as though he understands English as well as you or I, Robin Pyewacket Good-fellow leaps down from the top of one of the book-cases, holds his head high, and figure-eights through my legs.

I bend and scratch his head between his black-tufted ears. "You are the smartest, luckiest, most handsome cat in all the world."

"Re-ow." Thank you.

"And you were one hundred percent right about the Boy Scouts information."

"Ree-ow." Soft but condescending.

"Not sure why I ever doubted you, oh wise and powerful feline. Now, you take care of Grams, while I see how much influence I have over our local sheriff."

He affectionately butts his head against my leg, disappears behind a bookcase, and does not return.

I'll go ahead and assume he's vanished into one of his secret passages to the museum. No time to dawdle. I've got a burger and fries on my mind. Before I can make it out the front door, Twiggy returns from the Rare Books Loft. "Welcome to Bell, Book & Candle. Can I help you find something today, miss?"

Soaking in her pleasantries, I slowly turn like an evil villain in a spinning chair. "I'll have to remember to wear disguises more often, if this is the treatment I can expect."

Her cackle echoes off the tin-plated ceiling. "Well, I'll be hanged! You're never short on entertainment, doll. Where're you headed in that getup?"

"On my way to meet Silas and Erick at the diner. Hey, did you know Iris and my dad are half-siblings?"

"Everybody knows. Nobody talks about it. Your

Grams put the kibosh on that as soon as she found out Liliané was pregnant."

"Is their whole rivalry because of what happened with Max, in Paris?"

Twiggy widens her eyes in shock. "Who told you about that?"

"You forget, I've got a chatty ghost in my ear more often than not."

Twiggy's unmistakable cackle rings out once more. "Well, it's for a lotta reasons, not the least of which was Paris, but Liliané jumping into bed with Cal the week after his divorce from Isadora was final sure didn't help."

"What is it with that woman?"

"Don't you mean, what *was* it?"

"Didn't I tell you? I ran into her ghost out at the manor. She's as spiteful and narcissistic dead as she was alive."

"How'd she manage to stick around? Silas runnin' a school for lost souls?"

We share a laugh.

"No, hers is more of the standard unfinished business. Apparently, she was murdered."

Twiggy slaps her dungaree-clad thigh and hoots. "Well, it couldn't a happened to a nicer gal."

"That's what I'm starting to think. But I gotta get over to the diner. Wish me luck."

"Good luck, doll."

CHAPTER 17

WHEN I WALK into Myrtle's Diner not a head turns. Never have I felt so invisible. Silas is the first to take notice of my undercover arrival, and when I slide into the booth next to my lawyer, Erick gives me a friendly but distant smile.

He barely glances in my direction. "Silas, you didn't tell me anyone was joining us for lunch."

Silas chuckles almost silently into his bushy mustache.

"Well, I guess he didn't want to spoil the surprise, Sheriff."

Erick's jaw hangs slack and his eyes widen. "Wow! You're like a human chameleon."

"I'll take that as a compliment, I think."

"And who are you supposed to be this time?"

I throw on my timid, lisping voice and reply, "I'm Mr. Willoughby's assistant, Sheriff Harper."

He laughs until little tears leak out of the corners of his adorable peepers.

Looks like that's my cue. Operation influence the sheriff—Engage! "Silas and I were wondering what it would take to get Liliané's body exhumed?"

His laughter stops as suddenly as it started. He picks up his napkin, dabs at the corners of his eyes, and looks back and forth between my lawyer and me. "Please tell me this is more than one of your hunches."

Ignoring the jab at my sleuthing skills, I respond, "In light of Vassili's recent murder, I think the medical examiner needs to take another look at Liliané's body. I'm ninety-nine point nine percent sure she was murdered."

"Murdered? Her personal physician certified the cause of death as respiratory complications from her known history of emphysema. That doesn't sound like murder."

"What would you say if I told you she was smothered with a pillow and her attacker was scratched? There could be DNA under her fingernails."

Erick leans back, exhales, and shakes his head. "Look, you're gonna have to give me some kind of hard evidence. This entire story sounds manufactured. You're asking me to exhume a woman's body based on your claim that there *could be* DNA under her fingernails? I can't do that to the family. They've had two deaths in the space of a month. I can't go digging up bodies based on hearsay and flimsy theories."

Silas harrumphs and steeples his fingers. As he slowly bounces his chin on the tips of his pointers, I wait with bated breath. "Sheriff Harper, did you bring the crime scene photos we discussed?"

Before Erick can answer, Odell arrives and places a taco salad in front of Erick, liver and onions in front of Silas, and a cheeseburger joined by a mountain of crispy golden fries in front of me.

I look up in shock. "How did you know it was me?"

He winks as he sets down a bottle of Tabasco. "It's going to take more than a wig and some fake glasses to fool your surrogate grandpa." He raps his knuckles twice on the silver-flecked white Formica, turns and hesitates. "Come and see me on your way out." Without waiting for a reply, he returns to the kitchen.

I pick up a french fry and gush, "I think I love that man."

Erick smiles, but my extra senses pick up on a flash of jealousy. He slides a manila folder across the table.

Silas opens the folder and studies the images. He pushes the image of the rope knotted over the railing toward me. "Definitely a double bowline. Your *drawing* was surprisingly accurate." He takes mercy on me and keeps the photo of the *other* end of the rope to himself. "The knot on the other end is a figure-eight on a bight." He passes me the medical examiner's report. "The ME noted petechial hemorrhage, so regardless of the fact that the figure-eight is not a slip knot, the victim's own weight combined with the velocity of the fall would've resulted in strangulation."

Staring absently at the ME's report, I attempt to calculate the time that elapsed between the last time I saw Vassili alive and the blood-curdling scream that signaled his death. "The knot on the railing could've been tied in advance, but the one around his neck— That one was tied quickly, right before the killer pushed him overboard."

Silas nods and smooths his mustache with a thumb and forefinger. "That's a classic climbers knot, and definitely one of the basics which all Boy Scouts learn."

We exchange a meaningful glance.

"What are you two talking about?" Erick narrows his gaze.

"Today, we found out that Violet Barnes was the first female in Birch County to be admitted to the Boy Scouts." I cross my arms and lift my chin triumphantly.

Erick rubs a hand across his stubbled chin and shakes his head. "Violet? Now you think Violet killed Vassili? Yesterday you were certain it was Roman."

My shoulders sag, and I struggle for the right words to explain my information without revealing I've been chatting up Liliané's ghost.

He reaches across the table and twists his palm up invitingly.

With an exhale and a half smile, I place my hand in his.

He returns my weak attempt at a grin. "Can you at least take off the prop glasses? It's really hard to take you seriously."

Silas chuckles beside me, as I remove the glasses and set them on the table.

Taking a deep breath, I launch into my theory. "Look, it kind of makes sense. If Violet had a ticket to Mykonos, maybe Vassili was leading her on. He was secretly having an affair with Iris to keep one sister from contesting the will, while at the same time he's dangling the *promise* of a relationship in front of Violet to keep her from contesting the will."

Erick gives my hand a squeeze before he puts his arm across the back of the red-vinyl bench seat. "Okay, I'll play. What about Roman? He had as much claim to the fortune as Violet and Iris. How was Vassili keeping him from causing trouble?"

"Did you know most of Liliané's artwork is stolen?"

Silas clears his throat, and for the second time at this lunch Erick's jaw hangs open like a broken marionette.

"Well, it is. Liliané said Vassili would only want the artwork and he'd leave everything else to the kids. Maybe he promised the mansion to Roman, but then Roman found out about the affair with Iris and— Oh, I don't know. I suppose it could be Iris. For that matter, it could be Tom. I'm sure he would've been pretty upset to find out that his frigid wife was sleeping with his father-in-law!"

There's a strange silence at the table.

Silas is fastidiously engaged with his meal and Erick looks more confused than a freshman at the first day of college orientation.

"What? What did I say?"

"I wasn't aware that you were acquainted with Liliané Barnes. When exactly did you two meet?" Erick crosses his arms, and I'm momentarily distracted as I examine his biceps.

"I don't *exactly* remember. You're missing the point. I saw Roman fighting with Vassili earlier that night on the casino boat. Plus, what was the little black chunk of something at the crime scene?"

"Is it in the photo?" Erick moves toward the folder.

"I don't know. I saw something that night, though. I saw some chunk of— Violet's shoe! It was a broken heel tip. When I ran into her on the bow of the ship, she tripped a little. I asked her what happened to her shoe, and she didn't answer. And when I asked if she was the one who screamed, she kind of glared at me and hobbled away. So, maybe she broke her shoe trying to stop Roman from killing Vassili. Then she screamed when Roman pushed him over the railing."

Erick tilts his head back and forth as he weighs my theory. "That's sounding more believable than some of the other things you've come up with today. You said you saw Iris crying on the boat. How does that fit in?"

"Easy. She overheard the waitress bragging about hooking up with Vassili, and she probably realized her plan to get out from under Tom's thumb, pun intended, was kaput."

"And you're sure things were bad between Iris and Tom?"

"They have separate bedrooms at the manor. And Mrs. Charles said *no one* is ever allowed into Iris's room."

Erick grins smugly. "And yet you were in Iris's room."

I brush his comment away with a flick of my wrist. "You know what I mean. So, if Roman killed Vassili out of anger, either over being lied to or possibly to protect Iris, who killed Liliané? What if Roman killed her too?"

Still resisting getting on board my train of thought, Erick shakes his head. "What if no one killed her? What if her personal physician's report is accurate and you're asking me to exhume a woman's body for no reason?"

Exhaling in frustration, I grip the edge of the table with both hands. "I can't explain it, Erick, but I absolutely guarantee that Liliané was murdered. If you can think of any reason to get a judge to sign an exhumation order, I promise you will not regret it."

He takes a long slow sip of his soda pop before he replies. "That's a hefty gamble, Moon. A gamble that could cost me the next election."

I lean back and exhale. "You're worried about politics? I thought you were all about protecting your citizens and making sure justice is served."

"Sorry, thinking out loud. I have to consider my future, and my mother. I'm her sole caretaker."

Silas interjects. "Each of us has more to lose than to gain in this particular situation. However, I trust Mitzy's instincts, Sheriff. If it counts for anything, I put my full support behind her request to exhume the late Mrs. Barnes."

Erick sighs heavily. "Then I'm afraid I'm going to have to ask you to give me some legal guidance, Mr. Willoughby. You help me write up a convincing justification, and I'll talk to Judge Sandberg. He's a little more liberal and tends to fall on the side of law enforcement more often than not."

Silas nods solemnly. "I shall provide you with every ounce of my expertise."

With a nod of finality and a smile of satisfaction, I announce, "I need to get back to the bookshop and reorganize my murder wall. Keep me posted on the exhumation."

"Do you have to call it a murder wall? Could you call it your evidence organizer or maybe your snoop screen?" Erick's blue eyes plead adorably.

The three of us share a laugh and I shake my head. "It absolutely has to be called a murder wall. Every good crime-solving TV show or movie that I've ever seen in my life, always has a murder wall. It's part of my process. Sorry if I can't keep it all in my head, like you."

Erick laughs. "I don't keep it in my head. I have these nifty things called folders." At which point he reaches across the table, scoops up the crime scene photos, closes his folder, and gives Odell a salute as he exits the diner.

Turning to Silas, I roll my eyes around in my head like a crazy person. "I know, I said too much. I was so desperate to convince him. The bit about talking to Liliané slipped out before I could stop myself."

Silas nods and pats my shoulder comfortingly. "It may be time to tell your special friend the truth about your gifts."

"It's not. It's not time. He's a practical, logical law enforcement officer. If I tell him that I get weird visions, hear messages, and talk to ghosts, he'll run away faster than a jackrabbit being pursued by a coyote!"

"Isn't it a roadrunner that the coyote always pursues?"

"This isn't the time to update your pop-culture knowledge. But, yeah, it was a roadrunner in the cartoon. I was referring to real life in the Arizona desert." I slide out of the booth and start toward the kitchen.

Silas works his way across the bench seat behind me and hands me my fake eyewear. "Don't forget these, Dora."

Chuckling, I grab the glasses and slip them on. "I'm gonna check in with Odell, head back to the bookshop, and get changed into some regular old Mitzy clothes. Let me know what happens with the exhumation order?"

"Of course."

I duck into the kitchen. "Hey, Odell. What did you need?"

"Just wondering if you're the one who put a little stone cardinal on Myrtle Isadora's headstone?"

Before I can respond, my psychic senses flare with information. "You put the freesias in the vase?"

"Boy, you really do have the gift." He smiles. "They were her favorite." Nodding his head, he adds, "I'll keep your secret if you keep mine."

I can't stop myself from hugging this sweet curmudgeon. "Who am I gonna tell?"

His jaw clenches and the pain of loss seeps from his eyes. "Maybe you should have a séance. With your gift, you could probably talk to her for a minute or two."

My heart is cracking and my mouth is going to spill more than beans if I don't hightail it out of this diner. "I'll think about it. Thanks for visiting her. I know she appreciates— would appreciate it." Geez! I'm hopeless!

"See ya later, Mitzy."

"Bye, Odell."

I race back to the bookshop, determined not to think about Odell carefully tending Grams' grave. I've got to keep his secret, if at all possible.

Spoiler alert: Not possible.

Grams blasts through the bathroom door as I'm

getting into the shower. "He's the sweetest man on earth!"

"Myrtle Isadora! I mean, seriously! Boundaries, woman!" I grab a towel and clutch it to my unclothed person. "Boundaries! Mental and physical."

"What? Oh, sorry, dear. I heard about that wonderful man tending my grave and I forgot my manners. You should take a nice shower, and try to relax."

I open my mouth to speak, but choose to think my warning instead. *If you do not get out of my head and this bathroom at once, I will never wear another pair of designer heels as long as I live!*

And . . . Poof!

My ghost problem is handled.

The amazing, de-stressing effects of a hot shower, eucalyptus soap, and the softest most luxurious bath towels are hard to describe. I wrap a thick, oversized towel around my freshly scrubbed body, and wander out of the bathroom with a second towel over my head as I rub my hair dry.

Since thick Egyptian cotton covers my eyes, I sense the presence before I hear it. Whipping the towel from my eyes, I squeal, "Erick! What are you doing here? What are you doing in my apartment? Have you heard of a phone?"

His hand is firmly covering his eyes. "I'm so sorry. I'm not looking. I didn't see anything. Well, I saw the towel, but then I covered my eyes. I'm so sorry. I tried calling, but you didn't answer. And it's kind of important."

I fluff my hair back with my free hand and hold the second towel over the first. "All right. You're here now, so what's the emergency?"

"Mrs. Charles called the station and said that Violet hasn't been seen since Sunday, and Roman failed to show up for his tennis lesson and his massage appointment today."

I roll my eyes. "Oooh, the rich playboy missed his tennis lesson. That isn't an emergency."

"She also mentioned that Liliané's 9mm pistol is missing."

My mood ring burns and, without thinking, I look down. An image of Roman's face immediately followed by a gun, flashes through the swirling mist. "Do you think Roman might have kidnapped Violet? But why?"

"If your theory about him killing Vassili is right, and Violet is an eyewitness, he might be considering cutting his losses."

"Possibly? But why are you here?"

"No one knows where they went." He shifts his weight from one foot to the other and chews on his lip. "I happened to remember that one time, when you had a hunch about where Rory might be, and you were right. So can you maybe do your hunchy thing and figure out where Violet is?"

A warm feeling surges through my chest. He kind of admires me. "I'm happy to do my *hunchy* thing, but I'm gonna get dressed first and I'm coming with you to follow up on my hunch. Deal?"

Erick still has his hand firmly over both eyes. "I guess, but you'll have to wait in the car. Oh, and you should definitely get dressed."

I dive into my closet and quickly change into skinny jeans and a T-shirt that says, "Try Me" with a picture of a honey badger. There's no time for makeup or hair, and for a moment I toy with the idea of a wig. But, instead, grab something I hope I don't have to use from the depths of the wig drawer, slip it into the back of my waistband, and throw on a zip-front hoody to hide my secret.

Emerging from the closet, I smile when I see Erick's hand still over his eyes. "You can uncover your eyes now. I'm decent."

He removes his hand, but his cheeks are still tinged with the pink of embarrassment. "So what's your process? How do you get these hunches?"

"It's too hard to explain. Violet is at something called her 'forest fortress.' Any ideas?"

"Actually, I think so. Let's go. I'll explain on the way."

Once we're speeding along in the cruiser, he

continues, "One of Liliané's husbands owned several acres of land about thirty minutes outside of Pin Cherry. One year they held a huge fundraiser there for Mothers Against Drunk Driving. It was part of Liliané's community service, to get out of serving jail time for her third DUI arrest. But it definitely could be considered a forest fortress."

He keeps trying to get me to explain my hunches, but I use every trick in the book to expertly dodge his questions, including turning the interrogation back on him. "So what did Judge Sandberg say about the exhumation?"

"He was surprisingly open to it. He wasn't a fan of the way Liliané Barnes flouted the law during her lifetime, but he's also not a fan of letting murderers walk free. Silas and I presented a pretty convincing argument for connecting Vassili's murderer to Liliané's."

"That's great. Now what?"

"I sent Paulsen over to supervise the exhumation and handle chain of custody with the ME."

"What about the pregnancy test? Any word from the lab?"

"We should hear about that tomorrow."

He turns off the main road onto a single-track dirt road that winds through a forest of thick old-growth oak and elm.

Erick pulls over to the side of the road and turns off the engine.

"Why are you stopping? I don't see a fortress."

"If Roman has actually taken his sister prisoner, I don't want the sudden appearance of a squad car to push him over the edge. Hopefully, Violet is still alive. I want to keep the odds in her favor as long as possible."

"Copy that." I place a hand on my door handle.

"Hey, I said you had to wait in the car. That was our deal."

"Well, I'm not sitting in an abandoned car in the middle of the scary woods waiting for a murderer to pick me off. No way." I open my door and exit the vehicle.

"You never planned on waiting in the car, did you?" Erick looks over the top of the squad car with a mix of worry and admiration.

I put both hands up. "Guilty."

He shakes his head in defeat and leads the way.

When we reach the clearing, I'm gobsmacked. Forest fortress was an understatement. This is the kind of treehouse that adults dream of.

The massive structure seems to involve a minimum of ten huge trees. Each of the trees has got to be at least three hundred years old. The lower level is more open and has a seating area that would easily fit a hundred people.

As we get closer, I see the flooring is stone and there are built-in barbecues, sinks, and even refrigeration. Two curving stairways lead up to a second level.

Erick looks at me, points two fingers to his eyes, and motions for me to go up the far stairway.

Part of me wants to burst into laughter at the covert hand gestures, but the other part of me realizes that any screw up on my part could mean the difference between Violet living or dying. I nod and creep toward the back stairway. Moving slowly and carefully, I keep my weight toward the sturdy sides of each tread rather than the possibly squeaky middles. Unfortunately, my care slows me down too much, and before I reach the top of my staircase I hear Erick's commanding voice above.

"Drop the gun, Roman."

I hurry up the rest of the way and creep down the short hallway toward a central area, fit with beautiful organic furniture that seems to grow straight out of the floor. No time to admire the amazing construction or the vast size of this treehouse.

Violet is tied to a chair in the middle of the open space and, from my vantage point, I can see the tip of Roman's shaky hand pointing the 9mm in Violet's general direction, but I'm also able to observe

Erick in the background, inching along the edge of the room, moving in to flank Roman.

"Don't come any closer, Sheriff. I swear, I'll kill her."

"Take it easy, Roman. No one needs to kill anyone. We already know that you pushed Vassili over that railing. We don't need Violet's eyewitness testimony to bring charges. Killing her will only make your situation worse."

Roman's cold laughter turns my blood to ice in my veins. "Me? You think I killed Vassili?" He continues to laugh darkly and shakes the gun at his sister. "You've got everyone fooled, don't you? Weak little Violet." He scoffs and tries to steady the gun.

Violet's eyes are wide with terror and her mouth is gagged. She's twisting her head back and forth, desperate to free her voice. As she struggles, she catches sight of me sneaking in from the other direction. She falls absolutely still. Her eyes remain widened, but my extrasensory perceptions pick up on a deadly shift in her energy.

Most victims feel relief at the sight of a second rescuer, but she's sending off waves of a different kind. She's satisfied, vengeful . . . remorseless.

She resumes her struggle, but it's purely for show now. She's trying to drag her chair toward Roman—toward the gun.

"Stay back, Violet. You know I'll use this."

Erick takes a step closer to him. "Roman, I'm going to need you to put that gun down. I don't want to have to shoot you, but I'm not going to let you hurt Violet."

Violet throws herself into the role of victim, and crocodile tears spring from her eyes. She's scraping her way closer to Roman and she's working furiously at that gag. She finally gets her mouth free. "He did it. I saw him push Vassili over the railing." Sob. Sniffle.

Roman turns on his sister. "You liar. You did this to me. You were always the one who stole stuff. You're the one who broke mom's Ming vase. You got to blame everything on me."

Violet sobs dramatically. "He brought me here to kill me. He said he was gonna make sure I wouldn't talk."

She's doing everything she can to draw Erick's fire.

I hope I don't regret this.

I draw the gun my dad stole from Jimmy from my waistband, cock it, and fire.

Roman's gun whips out of his hand and lands on the floor.

He screams out in pain and sucks on his fingers.

I fire again.

The gun slides across the floor toward Erick.

"Don't struggle, Violet. Stay exactly where you

are." I aim my gun at the stolen jewelry pinned to her sweater and move in. "Nice emerald pin. Is that eighteenth century?"

Roman's face registers unmitigated shock.

Violet shows an impish grin. "So, Iris was right about you."

I'm not sure exactly what she plans to say, but I'm not about to take my gun off of her. My mood ring burns on my left hand and I look down in time to see a crystal clear image of the double figure-eight knot securing the rope around Vassili's neck. An involuntary shiver grips me.

Erick rushes in, picks up Roman's gun, and puts him in cuffs. "Nice shootin', Sundance. I'm sure you have a license for that."

"It's just like shootin' tuna off a paddle cactus back home in Boynton Canyon, Sheriff." I walk behind Violet and pull the gag back into her mouth.

She stares daggers at me and fights against the restraints.

Erick looks at me like I'm crazy. "What are you doing, Moon? Untie her. She's the victim here."

"I'm afraid I'll have to disagree. I'm pretty sure when the medical examiner finishes her report on Liliané's freshly exhumed body—" I pause for effect and lean toward Violet "—she's going to find Violet's DNA under the fingernails." I pull back the cardigan covering her sundress and reveal her shoulder. Deep scratches, somewhat healed, but no more than two weeks old, glare up angrily from her skin.

Erick shakes his head. "Violet Barnes, I'm placing you under arrest for suspicion of murder." He produces a second set of handcuffs, unties Violet, and then cuffs her. Surprisingly, he asks me to keep my gun on Roman while he secures Violet in the back of the cruiser.

While I'm alone with Liliané's only son, I make good use of my time. "When did you figure out Violet killed your mother?"

"When I found out she was carrying that scumbag Euro-trash's baby."

And suddenly, several pieces of the puzzle click into place.

CHAPTER 18

As ERICK NAVIGATES BACK to the station, I choose to take advantage of the fragile state of our two passengers and test out a couple of my hunches.

"So, how long has Iris been a rock climber?"

Violet narrows her gaze, and regardless of the fact that her gag has been removed, she makes no reply.

Roman steps in and returns the serve. "She only did it because Mother hated it. Every decision Iris ever made, including marrying that ludicrous yachtie, Tom, was to irritate our mother."

"Is she any good? I mean, does she still climb?"

Roman's voice carries a hint of pride. "She's one of the best climbers in the region. She's never done any free climbing, but she's an expert with the ropes. She holds the record for fastest clip in and rappel."

I glance toward Erick, and I sense his internal lightbulb flickering to life.

He turns and raises an eyebrow, and I nod. He grabs his radio and calls it in. "This is Sheriff Harper. Put out a BOLO for Iris Barnes-Becker and Tom Becker. The suspects are wanted in conjunction with the murders of Liliané and Vassili Barnes."

Violet finally finds her voice. "She was jealous of me. For once in my life I managed to outshine her. Vassili loved me. He was going to get all of my horrible mother's money, and take me to Greece." She kicks sharply at her brother. "Then I'd never have to see the likes of you two again."

Roman's adrenaline has definitely dissipated and the full weight of his decisions is beginning to sink in. "I'm sorry, V, but you shouldn't have killed Mother. I know she was cruel to you. She was cruel to all of us. Seeing us suffer was literally the only thing that made her happy. But you shouldn't have killed her."

Violet sighs and looks out the window. "She told me I was worthless. She said she named me Violet because she knew I'd never amount to anything. I'd always be alone, in a pot, on a windowsill. She said no one would ever love me. I wasn't enough. But Vassili loved me. And when I told him I was pregnant, he was so happy. Mother never would've let me keep it. She would've done something evil." She tears her gaze away from the road and stares pitifully at her brother. "You know her, Roman. She would've found a way to take my baby. I had to stop her." Her voice is barely a whisper now. "I had to stop her."

Roman looks at his broken, mentally unbalanced sister, and I feel the regret and compassion swirling up in his heart.

The stale cigarette smell from the Passageway of the Masters flickers to mind. "Roman, were you aware of your mother's art thefts?"

Most average humans would miss the shift in his energy. But thanks to my clairaudience, the word "accomplice" rings as clear as a bell inside my head. "Were you involved?"

Violet, the same woman he held at gunpoint moments ago, jumps to his defense. "It wasn't his choice. Mother used him. She said he looked like one of those British princes. She would pass him off at parties. He had to learn a British accent and everything. It's not his fault. You don't understand! Our mother was a tyrant."

"I understand more than you think, Violet. How did you kill her?"

Erick's eyes dart toward me. "Let me remind

you that you've been informed of your rights, Violet."

She ignores the sheriff's warning. "I smothered her with one of her stupid two-thousand-dollar down pillows! She wouldn't even spend money on contacts for me when I was in boarding school, but she would waste every cent of our inheritance on frivolous junk."

"And the will? Which one of you first found out about the will?"

Roman steps in. "That will caught us all by surprise. Mother used to threaten us with changing her will anytime we didn't do as she'd say. If she asked you to swindle an earl or a marquess out of a rare painting, you'd better hop to it or you'd find yourself disinherited. We all followed the rules. We all did what she said. None of us could have suspected such a cruel double-cross. Not even from her."

"Violet, what about you? You were literally sleeping with the enemy. Didn't Vassili give you any indication what your mother was planning?"

She doesn't respond, and Roman's frighteningly cold laugh returns. "Of course! That's the real reason you killed Mother. Vassili inherits everything. You convince Iris to kill Vassili. Bam! Your baby is the sole heir to the Barnes fortune. I can't believe I ever pitied you, Violet. You're as twisted and disgusting as our mother."

Violet attempts to attack Roman, with her hands cuffed behind her back.

Erick slams on the brakes and sends both their heads bouncing against the cage. "Settle down."

She whimpers, and Roman laughs. "No one's buying what you're selling, shrinking Violet."

We finally arrive at the police station and, as Erick and another deputy are removing the suspects from the backseat, an update comes over the radio. "Iris Barnes-Becker and Thomas Becker have been taken into custody at the airport. They were boarding a private plane chartered to the Maldives."

Erick looks over his shoulder at me and smiles. "Thanks again for the backup, Sundance."

"Anytime, Butch."

"Please, at least let me be Wyatt Earp."

I shake my head and chuckle.

Turning to walk down the block to my bookstore, the grating voice of Deputy Paulsen pierces the damp night air. "Moon, you gotta come in and make a statement."

Oh goody. How exactly am I going to tell this story and not mention my illegal firearm? "I need to run back and lock up the bookstore. I'll be down at the station to give my statement in about an hour."

Paulsen widens her stance and crosses her arms.

"Yeah. We know where you live. So don't think about runnin'."

I roll my eyes and hurry back to my apartment to hide the gun.

Uncharacteristically, Silas picks up on the first ring. After the requisite pleasantries, he questions my certainty regarding Violet's innocence in Vassili's murder.

"Absolutely certain. Iris is an expert rock climber. According to Roman, she holds some records—probably in knot tying as well as climbing."

"Ah, the missing piece."

"Yep. I'm on my way to the bookstore. My dad's back from his trip and he wants to catch me up on a few things."

Silas says his goodbyes, and my steps take an unhurried pace toward the lakeshore. Standing atop the bluff, at the edge of the cul-de-sac, I gaze out over the blue-grey waters. Family can be so many things. Good things. Bad things. And even though death is part of the cycle of life, I wish murder wasn't.

From everything I've learned, Liliané Barnes was not a nice woman and, by all accounts, a terrible mother. Maybe it's true what they say, about the good dying young. My mother was the best, and fate took her from me far too soon. As I turn back toward the bookshop, I end up walking past the entrance and continuing down the block to the Duncan Restorative Justice Foundation.

Ducking down the alleyway, I ring the bell beside my father's metal door.

Jacob smiles broadly as he opens it to greet me. "I was hoping it was gonna be you." He pulls me into a warm hug.

I return the affection. "Hey, how was your trip?"

His grin conceals something, and I can absolutely tell there's a current of excitement underneath his cool exterior.

"Come on up to the apartment and I'll catch you up."

We cross the broad entryway and I gaze up at the statue of my Grandpa Cal. Why on earth would he have married Liliané Barnes? I suppose it was a different time. And he was more concerned about doing the right thing and being a father to Iris. Unfortunately, he never got the opportunity.

We step into the elevator, and my dad waves his key card in front of the reader to activate the penthouse button.

As the elevator doors slide open, several new pieces of furniture in the apartment are revealed, along with a beautiful abstract painting I don't remember seeing before.

"I thought you were on a fundraising trip? What's with all the new digs?"

He turns and smiles nervously. "That's what I was going to tell you. Most of the trip was for the foundation, but Amaryllis met me in Chicago this past weekend and, well, I proposed. Are you okay with that?"

His question utterly shocks me. We haven't even known each other a year, and the fact that he would be concerned about my feelings regarding his personal relationships is sweet but totally unnecessary. "Dad, I'm super happy for you. Amaryllis is wonderful, and she shares your passion for the foundation. I think you guys make a great couple." I choose to keep the twinge of sorrow to myself. I just found him and now I could lose him all over again . . . Although, to be fair, he does live right across the alley, and *her* furniture in *his* penthouse seems to indicate this will be their post-nuptial residence. Maybe I need to get over myself.

"Well, that's a load off."

"Did you honestly think I wouldn't be happy for you?"

"I don't know what I thought. I still feel so bad that I missed out on your life. That your mom never told me about you. That I made bad choices and lost the opportunity . . ."

Rushing over, I hug him tightly. "Look, Dad,

after my recent experience with the insane, murderous Barnes family— I'm willing to be pretty flexible to make sure we don't blow our second chance."

He pulls away and tilts his head. "I'm sure you found out about Iris."

"Yeah, that was a heck of a shocker."

"Sorry about the surprise. I learned pretty early in life that it wasn't a good idea to cross Isadora Duncan."

We chuckle and tense up for a moment, almost expecting her to pop in.

"She's not any easier to deal with in the afterlife, I can assure you. But I do need to get back to the apartment and get Grams up to speed." Pausing at the elevator, I turn. "Breakfast tomorrow? You can give me pointers for my dinner date with Erick tomorrow night."

Jacob smiles. "Sounds great. No spoilers, but I only have one tip: have fun and don't stay out too late. I'll be pacing in front of my new sofa until I see your light come on."

I roll my eyes. "Oh, brother. See ya tomorrow."

As soon as I get back to the apartment, I fill Grams in on all the juicy details she's dying to hear, and some of the procedural stuff she couldn't care less about.

"Silas said they're going to hire a forensic accountant, an art appraiser and some other expert whose title I've forgotten, to trace the artwork back to its original owners. Everything that can be properly returned, will be, and the rest will be placed in museums around the country."

"I knew she was up to something. I told you!"

"Yes, Grams. You get full credit for assuming Liliané was probably up to no good. She was *in fact* up to no good."

She follows me into the closet. "You still have that gun? You're keeping it?"

"Look, I most likely saved someone's life, and I definitely impressed Erick. I'm keeping it for now."

"I think you should talk to your father—"

"Funny you should mention Jacob." I let her stew in her own dimension while I tuck the gun in the back of a drawer. "He's getting married."

Ghost-ma freeze-frames and flickers in and out of existence. "What? When?"

"I didn't ask. He told me that he proposed to Amaryllis in Chicago this past weekend."

Glistening tears spring from her eyes.

"Grams? What's wrong? Aren't you happy for him?"

"I won't be there." She snuffles loudly. "My only child is finally getting married and I can't be there."

"Two things: first, I swear I will find a way to get a hanky into the afterlife; and, lastly, it's not about you. Dad's getting married and your first thought should be how wonderful it is that he's rebuilding his life. All right?"

Her tears subside, but I can tell she's still pouting.

"How about I let you pick out an outfit for my date with Erick tomorrow night? Will that help?"

Her aura instantly sparkles. "Outta my way!" She pretends to shoo me out of the closet.

Leaving her to her own devices, I wander off to find a snack and make sure Pyewacket has been properly praised for his role in the case.

CHAPTER 19

THIS FINAL TRIP to the Barnes estate is not necessarily against my will, but against my better judgment.

Silas insists that I give Liliané the closure that she needs and ensure that she crosses over.

While I'm not entirely sure a woman like her deserves either of those things, I shudder to think what her anger, resentment, and vindictive nature could accomplish with centuries of ghost-life at her disposal.

So I've agreed to return to the manor on the conditions that I'm allowed to drive my Jeep and that I'm allowed to return as Mitzy Moon, not Ms. Donaldson the mousy assistant or Dora the violent maid.

The size and obsessive upkeep of the estate fail

to impress. Once you've had as thorough a look behind the grandeur as I have, appearances no longer
hold any sway.

I might've grown-up a poor orphan, but at least
I learned to put people before money.

As we pull up in front of the ornate main entrance, the door opens and the doorman performs
his standard no-eye-contact duties.

"Looks like Mrs. Charles got the coup under
control."

Silas chuckles and swipes at a portion of the
dust on his briefcase. "I'm not sure whether you realize how much you see, Mizithra."

Shrugging my shoulders, I scrunch up my face.
"I mean, we both saw him walk out and open the
door. Right? Last time we were here the whole
place was in an uproar."

"Indeed. And exactly as you stated, Mrs.
Charles calmed the unrest and put the household
right."

Turning off the ignition, I pocket the key and
reach for the door handle, before it hits me. "Hold
on. Are you offering her the caretaker position?"

Silas smiles like a rarely proud, but pleasantly
surprised to be so, mentor. "Your powers are coming
along nicely."

"That was simply basic observation, I think." I
open my door, step onto the crushed oyster-shell

driveway, and lean back inside the vehicle. "Do you think it was my powers? Maybe it's blurring together and I don't really notice whether it's observation or extrasensory."

He nods and smooths his grey mustache with a thumb and forefinger. "Regardless of the source, your observation was accurate. Perhaps it is more important to focus on the positive outcome. Now, we had best make haste to the library, before this dutiful footman releases all the cold air in the mansion."

Silas shuffles through the entryway and Mrs. Charles greets him with an uncharacteristic smile.

I stop and turn to the doorman. "Hello. I'm Mitzy Moon. What's your name?"

His focus flounders and his eyes dart toward Mrs. Charles.

"Oh, I can assure you she's going to be busy for quite a while. Do you enjoy your work?" I offer a friendly smile.

His stern features soften. "I'm called Clyde. Came with the house."

His voice is a little slow and thick. I get the feeling his life is best managed through routine. "Did Mrs. Barnes hire you?"

"No, miss." His eyes dart again toward the now empty foyer, and he leans toward me. "My mother got me the job, miss."

My eyes widen in surprise. Mrs. Charles has a son, and apparently she cares for him. "Well, I'm very pleased to see you manning the door. We plan to have a number of fundraisers in this fine home over the coming years, and I certainly hope you will do us the honor of opening the door for all of our wonderful guests."

He smiles broadly and nods his head. "I can do that, miss. I can do that."

Shaking his hand, and patting him firmly on the shoulder, I take my leave and hurry upstairs to the Cerulean Bath.

Before I settle in to perform my "medium" duties, it occurs to me that the ghost in residence is likely sulking in her room.

Up another flight of stairs to the third floor. I try the doorknob to Liliané's quarters.

Locked.

Good thing I brought my pilfered key.

Slipping the key into the lock, opening the door, and securing it behind me, I begin my search. "Liliané? Liliané, I have a bunch of news to share."

She materializes in a disgraceful lump in the middle of the bed. "I've heard the staff gossiping. My horrible, ungrateful children." Her unglamorous sobs echo off the high ceilings.

"I'll be right back." Rushing down the hallway, I

stick my head into each room until I find what I'm looking for.

Success.

Ice, gin, dry vermouth—shake briskly with ice, drain into a crystal martini glass, and garnish with two olives on a cocktail stick. Oops, don't forget the dash of olive brine to make it dirty.

Heading back to the room as quickly as I can without spilling the precious liquid, I once again lock the door behind me.

Back inside, I extend the glass toward my sobbing ghost. "Liliané, I brought you a present."

She lifts her head dramatically. "Oh, darling. You are an absolute angel!"

She attempts to take the glass from me, but she has none of the skill that Grams possesses. She's utterly unable to grip the finely wrought stem.

"Just my luck. I finally find a waitress who can make a proper drink, and I am powerless to consume it. I thought death would be a glorious celebration of my earthly achievements; instead I feel more useless than the second mistress." She falls back against the bed and whimpers.

"Would you rather move on? Would you rather see what the afterlife holds for you on the other side of the veil?"

She surges upward through the canopy on her bed toward the ceiling. "You know I would. I could be reunited with *some* of my favorite husbands. And I could console that poor little lamb, Vassili."

"Then I have some good news. Your unfinished business is finished."

"What are you saying, darling?"

"I'm saying the rumors are true, assuming you heard the right rumors. Violet is the one who killed you. I saw the scratches you left on her shoulder and the emerald pin on her cardigan."

Rather than anger, Liliané seems delighted. "Oh, my darling shrinking Violet. She finally found her spine! What more could a mother want?"

I can think of eight or ten things, but I'm certainly not going to mention them to Liliané. "Iris is being charged with Vassili's murder, and Roman will be charged with kidnapping and the attempted murder of Violet, but, considering she was a wanted felon, I'm assuming the jury will go fairly easy on him."

"Oh, especially if he uses that British accent. It's so posh. No one would believe he could be guilty of anything." Liliané laughs in a self-aggrandizing manner and floats toward me. "And what about Tom? What happens to that nasty, handsy little man?"

"It's my understanding that he's selling the yacht locally and taking a sailboat through the canals to a buyer on the Atlantic coast. Then he's hopping a plane to somewhere in the South Pacific and plans to live aboard his other sailboat. So, if he was involved in any way, he'll soon be beyond the reach of the authorities."

"Darn! I was really hoping he'd suffer retribution, at least for the torture he put Iris through."

"Sorry we let that one slip through the cracks, Liliané." I openly roll my eyes. "Now, I'm going to drink this martini and toast your transmutation to the afterlife."

She examines her many pendants, brooches, and rings. "Did you bring me the emerald pin?"

"Sadly, that will have to stay in evidence until after Violet's trial. Maybe it could be a christening gift for your grandchild?"

Ignoring my suggestion of acknowledging her growing family tree, she instead takes the opportunity to put me in my place. "I told you it wasn't Iris who got knocked up. Oh, and the Barnes family doesn't *do* religion." Still salty about her brooch, she pouts into her manicured fingers. "Well, you did what you could, darling."

And with that, I raise my glass. "Liliané Barnes, here's to your afterlife."

She beams with pride.

Removing the cocktail stick with the two olives, I down the martini in one gulp, and smile. "So long."

Her image flickers violently and I sense her resisting.

I eat one of the olives and her signal grows fainter.

A voice that sounds like it's coming from the bottom of a well calls out to me, "Maybe I should stay. I could learn to be a better ghost."

"I hear Hell has a presidential suite reserved for you, *darling*." And with that, I pop the last olive in my mouth and flick the drops of gin remaining in the bottom of the martini glass at her specter.

There's a sizzle and a POP, as she vanishes from this plane of existence.

Who would've thought? Alchemical cocktails . . . Sounds like a bar I'd visit.

Turning to leave the room, I come face-to-face with the very unhappy face of Mrs. Charles, dangling her "only" key. "And what do you think you're doing in here, young lady?"

"I was on a mission." I brandish the martini glass. "I was giving Liliané a proper sendoff. Her rotten children certainly failed in that department." Clearly, the gin is already kicking in.

Mrs. Charles uncrosses her arms and blinks back tears. "That's the sweetest thing I've ever heard uttered in this house."

Handing her the martini glass, I stagger my way

back downstairs to an amused Silas pacing under the seven-tiered chandelier.

"Was your mission a success, Mitzy?"

Bowing clumsily, I trip down the last couple of stairs and steady myself on the banister. "Indeed, Mr. Willoughby. I sent another one home." My voice sounds loud in my own head.

Silas scoops an arm around me and shushes me all the way back to the Jeep.

"Why don't you give me the keys? You collect yourself in the passenger seat and I'll transport you safely back to the bookstore."

I hop into the Jeep and buckle my seatbelt. "Good, 'cuz I have a date with a very handsome sheriff tonight. He really likes me."

Silas chuckles quietly as he drives me home.

He thinks his voice is too soft for me to hear, but he's forgetting that I got skills. "I believe he truly does, Miss Moon."

CHAPTER 20

ERICK IS TAKING me to dinner at a cute little Italian restaurant, over on Gunnison Avenue, near the veterinary clinic. Grams has been in the closet since yesterday searching for the perfect dress.

"Just remember, I'm going to be eating pasta. I need a dress with a little room for expansion, if you know what I mean."

Grams chuckles. "You're a corker! How do you feel about ruffles?"

"I feel like I'll probably hate them, so can you be more specific?" I walk into the closet and smile. The dress she has laid on the padded mahogany bench in the center definitely hits all the right notes. It's an adorable sundress. It's not too short or too long, should hit about mid-thigh, and the ruffles are vertical, almost like rows of tiny bells.

In combination with the A-line cut, the ruffles should definitely enhance my bottom-heavy figure.

Not to mention that the color palette of greens, teal blues, and a range of purples is sort of the perfect girly camouflage for a pasta dinner. Potential drips of sauce will disappear, and my starch-bloated belly will be well hidden. "You've got yourself a deal, on one condition."

"Don't even say it!" Grams slips an utterly breathtaking pair of silver strappy shoes off the shelf. "I know you prefer a lower heel, dear, but these are chunky and stable. And they're barely three- or four-inch heels."

Not her first ghostly lie of the day and certainly not her last. The heels are easily five or six inches, but they are chunky, and the strappy sandals will look amazing with the dress.

"All right. You win."

She giggles like a schoolgirl and claps her ethereal hands soundlessly together. "What do you think his surprise is?"

"I'm going to pretend you didn't ask me that. I'm sure I never told you anything about a surprise, so the only way you'd have any knowledge of said surprise is by sneaking your way into my thoughts!"

"Not entirely true, dear. You were talking in your sleep last night. So your lips were moving, and based on our rules . . ." She lifts her sparkly hands in surrender.

"Fine. But I have no idea what the surprise is, so there's nothing to tell."

"Haven't you used your gifts to scoop in and get some information?"

"Absolutely not! That feels like it would be a betrayal. Erick doesn't know about my powers, so he certainly hasn't given me permission to use them on him."

She arches one brow. "But you've done it before."

"Not on purpose, and not for personal gain."

Grams snickers. "If that's what we're telling ourselves."

Choosing to completely ignore her annoying teasing, I put on more makeup than usual, even adding eyeliner and a hint of shadow.

Ghost-ma attempts to stifle her joyous squeal in the other room.

A couple of spins around the curling wand and I'm ready to get dressed.

The doorbell at the alley door rings right as I'm buckling the final strap on my shoes. "Perfect timing."

As I reach the bottom of the wrought-iron circular staircase, I choose not to tempt fate with some fumbled effort to step over the chain. I unhook the

"No Admittance" chain and brazenly leave it unhooked.

The doorbell sounds again and I smile. Seems like he might be a little bit excited about our date. I open the door, with a hand on my hip, and pretend to frown. "Am I not worth waiting for, Sheriff Harper?"

Erick smiles and takes a moment to appreciate the view. "You're always worth the wait, but I skipped lunch. So you can blame my stomach for the double-tap."

"Copy that." With my history of food-related priorities, far be it from me to judge the gorgeous Erick Harper for letting his appetite make a decision.

On the short drive over to Angelo and Vinci's, I am powerless to ignore the waves of emotion rolling off my date. My senses pick up that he is mostly filled with anticipation, but every now and then there's a strange stabbing pain. I promised myself I would only use my powers for good. Maybe if I repeat this enough times, I can prevent myself from snooping around his insides with my gifts.

Thankfully the restaurant sweeps into view, complete with an Italian flag out front and red and green neon lights announcing, *Angelo and Vinci's Italian Ristorante*.

As soon as the patrol car comes to a stop, I place my hand on the door.

Erick reaches across and gently taps my knee.

I'm filled with tingles and I turn in confusion.

"Would you mind sitting tight while I come around and open your door?"

The modern girl in me feels a flash of feminist resistance, but deep down I know Erick understands that I'm capable of taking care of myself. It's a polite gesture and it means something to him. Maybe mutual respect is the only thing at stake. "No problem. Thanks for asking."

He smiles and steps out of the vehicle.

As he rounds the front of the vehicle, I take a long sip of the tall drink of water that is Erick Harper. He's wearing a very nice pair of blue hand-sanded jeans and a fitted button-down shirt that emphasizes his broad shoulders and tapered waist. It's also a thrill to see that he let his hair hang a little looser and more casual for our date. No pomade.

He opens my door and offers his hand.

Placing my hand in his, I have to catch my breath as he pulls me up quickly and plants a little kiss on my cheek. The citrus-woodsy smell that will always represent him, in my mind, makes me a little weak in the knees.

Holding my hand softly in his, he guides me toward the restaurant.

Outside the door, I drag my feet.

He turns. "Is something wrong?"

"Not exactly."

His grin spreads slowly. "Ask away."

"I need to clarify a couple things and then I promise I won't talk about murder, or the Barnes psychos, for the rest of the night."

His smile is pinched and his mood isn't as light as I'd hoped.

"So, you questioned Iris again?"

"Yes, with her lawyer present."

"Did she confess?"

"She painted quite a different picture from the one Violet was selling."

I rub my hands together eagerly. "Do tell."

"According to Iris, she was led to believe the relationship between Violet and Vassili was not consensual."

"You mean— Oh, geez. So why was Iris flirting with Vassili if she thought he was a sexual predator?"

"Apparently, she was trying to bait him into attacking her. But when she heard about him sleeping with the waitress on the cruise . . . She went a different direction."

"Vengeful angel? She decided to kill the man who knocked up her sister against her will?"

Erick rubs his stubbled chin. "Not exactly. She

claims that Violet took that pregnancy test on Saturday. She had no way of knowing about the baby on Friday."

A flash of knowing smacks unbidden into my consciousness. "But Violet knew. She had morning sickness on the cruise. That test she took with Iris had to be the second test. Otherwise, why would she have killed her mother to save the baby?"

He shakes his head. "Maybe. But I think Violet killed her mother so she could run away with Vassili. The trip to Mykonos was booked before Violet could've known about the baby. I think once she found out she was pregnant, she wanted to get rid of Vassili so—"

"So her kid would be the sole heir!" I smack my hands together. "Sorry. It would be genius if it weren't so evil."

"Yeah. What a messed up family." Erick sighs heavily.

"Is there any chance you can get DNA from the figure-eight knot on the rope?" I offer him a wistful half smile.

"Like you said that night, everyone was wearing gloves, so it's pretty unlikely."

I raise my finger eagerly. "But we know the knot had to be tied very fast. If Violet was attempting to hold Vassili's arms and Iris was going for a record-breaking, five-second knot time—she would've used her bare hands."

He nods. "I hope you're right. We could definitely use some hard evidence to tie Iris to the murder weapon—"

"No pun intended." I chuckle shamelessly.

Erick grins and grips the handle of the restaurant's front door. "Time for our date?"

Unable to stop myself, I blurt, "Hey, did you know my dad was related to Iris?"

He avoids eye contact. "I didn't have proof or anything, but the timeline and their ages made a pretty convincing argument."

Shaking my head, I reach out and grip his hand. "All right, enough about messed up families and weird relations, and murdering psychopaths." I look into his adorable eyes. "Our date officially starts now."

He squeezes my hand and we walk inside.

The hostess takes us to our table, hands us our menus, and informs us that the restaurant's fascinating origin story is printed on the back of the menu.

"Well, now I have to read that story." I give Erick a wink as I flip over my menu.

According to the *legend*, this place used to be a big playhouse for local community theater. But a larger, more modern facility opened in Broken

Rock, and this one was boarded up—until two Italian brothers retired to the area from Chicago. They couldn't resist the opportunity to start a new ristorante and they filled the theater-turned-eatery with old props, scenery, costumes, masks, and a plethora of cheap, imitation-marble statues. The overall effect is probably garish in the pure light of day, but in the dim candlelight, with strings of twinkling Christmas lights winding their way up and down the walls, it actually feels magical.

As I finish reading the story and taking in the scenery, it's impossible to ignore that Erick's general vibe has shifted toward tense. "Is anything wrong?"

His eyes widen self-consciously. "Is it that obvious?"

A little knot tightens in my stomach. I knew things in my life were too good to be true. My luck with men is finally about to return to its usual pattern of epic fails. "Not at all. Just wondered."

His hand shoots across the table and he grips my fingers. "I was going to wait until after we—"

"Can I get either of you a drink this evening?"

Classic server's timing.

Her eyes dart back and forth between us, utterly clueless to what she may have interrupted.

"Can we get a bottle of Chianti, and two waters?"

"Right away, Sheriff."

Despite the tension, I have to chuckle. "Looks like we'll have to go out to dinner in another county if we want any real privacy."

His jaw clenches. "Yeah, I should've thought of that."

Well, now I'm even more nervous. "You were saying?"

He grips my hand again. "I was going to wait until after dinner to give you this, but— No, I think I should wait."

"What's going on? Give me what?"

"I kind of got you a present, but it ended up being more complicated than I thought."

I lean toward him and smile. "Um, there's pretty much no way I'm going to be able to eat anything until I get the rest of the story."

He nods and withdraws his hand as the server lays down a basket of breadsticks and scurries away.

"Understood. Let me power down one of these breadsticks, and then we'll get into it."

I wave down our server and ask, "Can I get a glass of red wine. Bring the bottle of Chianti whenever you get around to it. I'll take a glass of anything you have open, right away."

Her eyes widen with concern and she looks back and forth between Erick and me. "Right away, miss."

Erick finishes one breadstick and begins on the

second, as the server slides my wine in front of me.

Picking up the glass of dark red liquid, I raise it in a halfhearted toast to Erick, and down the glass in one lengthy gulp. "Ready when you are, Sheriff."

He lays a manila envelope on the table.

Weird. I don't remember seeing him carry that in, he must've had it tucked under his—Better not think about what may or may not be under his shirt. "What's this?" I reach for the envelope.

He lays a hand on mine. "Please remember, I honestly meant it as a gift."

The hairs on the back of my neck rise like the hackles of a cat. "Understood." I take the envelope, fold up the clasp, and start to dump the contents onto the table. When the first item hits the white tablecloth, my heart stops beating and I drop the envelope. "That's—"

"Have you guys decided what you'd like to order, or would you like to hear the specials?"

I stare at Erick as my eyes fill with tears.

"We'll both have the lasagna and that's all."

The server glances at me for a split second, but I'm sure my tears drive her away faster than anything else.

Picking up the necklace from the table, I hold it in the palm of my hand as though it's as fragile as a bird's egg. "This was my mother's. How did you get this?"

"I wanted you to have a picture or something. I know you were only eleven when she passed away, and since you went into the foster system, I thought maybe no one had ever collected her personal effects. I contacted the Maricopa County Sheriff to see if I could get a favor."

I look at the envelope and my stomach churns. "If this is the good part, I'm not sure I want to dump out the rest."

"I wasn't sure I should even give it to you. But it didn't feel right to hide the truth."

I look back down at the sterling silver dream catcher with its three sterling silver feathers and the tiny amethyst crystal at its center. "My mother wore this every day. Of course she would've been wearing it the day of the accident. I totally forgot." The emotions are bubbling so close to the surface, I really don't want to make a scene in this restaurant.

Erick takes a look at my red-rimmed eyes. "It was stupid of me to give this to you in public. Let me go ask them to package everything to-go and we can look through the rest of this in your apartment."

I nod immediately, but as soon as he leaves the table my brain processes what he actually said. "In my apartment." Do I want Erick Harper in my apartment? I mean, my apartment is basically just my bedroom. Not sure if I can actually handle that. My knotted stomach tries to flip-flop excitedly, but that sensation brings a wave of nausea. The mood ring tingles icily on my left hand, but I refuse to look at it. I'm barely holding it together as it is. If I look down and see my mom's face, I will absolutely lose it.

He returns to the table. "Good news. Angelo's son Dante is working tonight and he said he'll deliver it. He's a good kid. He's gonna deliver the Chianti too." Erick scoops up the envelope, but hesitates as he looks at the necklace in my hand. "Would you like to put it on?"

I gaze up at him and smile. "Yeah, I think I would."

He gently takes the necklace from my hand and clasps it around my neck. He offers me his hand and helps me out of the chair, grabs the manila envelope, and leads me out to the squad car.

In a few minutes we're back at the bookshop and I'm opening the alleyway door.

Unfortunately, Grams has been spinning in ghost-swirls since I left and races toward me like an anxious parent. "What's wrong, Mitzy? You got back so soon. Did you fight?"

I press my lips together as hard as I can to keep from speaking out loud and send Grams a telepathic message. *Erick gave me a really amazing gift, but he has some information about my mom, and I don't think it's good. Can you please go work on your memoirs in the museum and absolutely promise not to come back to the apartment tonight?*

Shimmering tears spring to her eyes and she nods her head rapidly. "I promise, dear, but I'm checking on you first thing in the morning."

I nod my head slightly and lean on Erick as he guides me to the staircase. We walk across the Rare Books Loft in silence. The neat rows of oak desks and the individual brass reading lamps seem especially hushed in the twilight.

Reaching up, I pull the candle handle.

He lets out a low whistle as the bookcase slides open and reveals my hidden apartment. "Never ceases to impress."

I smile wanly and plop down on the settee.

Erick lays the manila envelope on the coffee table. "Can I get you a glass of water or something stronger?"

"I don't think we actually have anything stronger. Grams is—was a recovering alcoholic. But a glass of water would actually be great."

He disappears downstairs to retrieve my simple beverage, and I unbuckle my strappy silver heels and kick them off onto the floor.

Sitting perfectly still, I stare at the dangerous envelope as though it were a coiled rattlesnake, and another wave of nausea passes over me.

Erick returns with a glass of water, as the alley

doorbell rings. "I'll get that. You sit tight."

Taking the glass of water, I nod my thanks.

He returns moments later with our lasagna, another batch of breadsticks, and two bottles of Chianti.

"Either they took us for a couple of lushes, or someone told them to push the wine."

I chuckle lightly in spite of the swirling in my stomach.

He runs back downstairs to retrieve silverware and glasses.

When he returns, I stare at the food and shake my head in dismay. "Not sure if I can eat."

Erick's eyes widen. "Should I call a doctor?"

His joke eases the tension, and after the brief laughter, I recover my ability to enjoy food.

Half a serving of lasagna and a breadstick later, I pour my second glass of wine. "I'm ready for the rest of the story. And whatever the rest of the story is, this was the kindest thing anyone has ever done for me. And I mean ever, including all of this." I gesture to the swanky apartment. "To have this necklace . . . I don't know if I'll ever be able to express how much it means to me." Tears trickle down my cheeks, and Erick jumps up and runs into my bathroom before I can stop him.

He returns with a box of tissues and a smirk. "Maybe you should hire your own maid."

I chuckle through my tears. "Maybe you should mind your own business."

He takes a seat on the floor and slides the envelope toward me. "Are you ready?"

"I'm ready."

He opens the envelope, pulls out the papers and begins his story.

"This was the only photo in the packet. It was from her driver's license, I kind of had it enlarged. But honestly, I've never seen anyone take such a great driver's license picture."

I take the picture and stare into the beautiful dark eyes that raised me for eleven years. "I've already forgotten so much. This photo is priceless. Thank you." Leaning down, I kiss him as more tears flood my cheeks.

He hands me another tissue and sighs. "Now for the not so good."

I steel my insides for the bad news.

"According to the coroner's report, your mother's death wasn't an accident."

"What? Her car was hit by a commuter train." I place a hand over my mouth and shake my head. "She pulled in front of the train on purpose? Are you saying she committed suicide?"

Erick shakes his head slowly. "She was murdered. The crash was an attempt to cover up any evidence that would point to the murder."

I jolt backward against the over-stuffed settee. My whole world is spinning out of control and my mood ring is threatening to sear the flesh off my left hand. I don't dare risk a glance.

"But why? She was a good person. Why?" All of the shock, horror, and injustice of the first moment I heard about my mother's death comes flooding back.

Erick slips onto the settee next to me and places an arm around my shoulders. "Your mother was working as a confidential informant for the Phoenix Metro Police Department."

My whole body feels as cold as ice. I'm sure I'm not breathing, and it almost feels like my heart has stopped beating as well. "But who murdered her?"

He swallows, and I can feel him struggling with his decision.

"You have to tell me. I mean, I'll read through the papers—I'll find out. You have to tell me. Who killed my mother?"

His blue-grey eyes get a little misty and he whispers, "It's unsolved. A cold case."

My shock and sorrow explode into rage. I jump off the couch and stare at him indignantly. "Unsolved? The person who murdered my mother is walking free?" I pace in front of the windows, balling my hands up into fists.

A small voice attempts to reach through my

fury. "I have a lot of vacation days saved up that I've never taken."

The utter incoherence of his statement stops me in my tracks. "What?"

He stands, walks toward me, and pulls me into an embrace. "I have a lot of vacation that I haven't taken. When do you want to leave?"

As the true meaning of his words hits my soul, I can no longer hold back the tears. I collapse onto his chest and let myself cry for all the things that I will never know and all the years that I was robbed of the truth.

Once I finish feeling sorry for myself, I swipe away my tears. "And now *this* is the kindest, most amazing thing that anyone has ever done for me. Careful, Sheriff, you're setting a dangerous precedent."

"I'm happy to do it. Somebody has to keep the new Sundance Kid out of the hoosegow."

I melt into his arms and let our laughter push away the sadness.

Looks like it's time for Mitzy Moon to return to the Southwest. Me and my posse—of one—are gonna distribute some Old West justice.

Yee-haw!

End of Book 8

A NOTE FROM TRIXIE

Jackpot! Another case solved! I'll keep writing them if you keep reading . . .

The best part of "living" in Pin Cherry Harbor continues to be feedback from my early readers. Thank you to my alpha readers/cheerleaders, Angel and Michael. HUGE thanks to my fantastic beta readers who continue to give me extremely useful and honest feedback: Veronica McIntyre, Renee Arthur, and Nadine Peterse-Vrijhof. And big "small town" hugs to the world's best ARC Team – Trixie's Mystery ARC Detectives!

A heartfelt bow of gratitude to my editor, Philip Newey. I always look forward to Philip's straight-forward, no-nonsense feedback. I would also like to give another long overdue THANK YOU to Brooke for her tireless proofreading! Any errors are my own, as my outdated version of Word insists on showing me only what it likes and when it feels so moved.

You can all thank my near death experience rock climbing in an abandoned quarry for my obsession with knots.

Also, quick thanks to my in house "test dummy" for letting me tie a rope around your neck, until I could get my time under five seconds!

I'm currently writing book ten in the Mitzy Moon Mysteries series, and I think I may just live in Pin Cherry Harbor forever. Mitzy, Grams, and Pyewacket got into plenty of trouble in book one, *Fries and Alibis*. But I'd have to say that book three, *Wings and Broken Things*, is when most readers say the series becomes unputdownable.

I hope you'll continue to hang out with us.

Trixie Silvertale (July 2020)

Mitzy Moon Mysteries 9

A touching gift. A shocking truth. Can this psychic sleuth solve a decade-old murder?

Mitzy Moon is happy to leave her painful past buried. But a thoughtful present turns her world upside down and forces her to abandon Ghost-ma and her fiendish feline to search for answers in the Southwest. Turns out her mom's death was no accident, and proving it could be the last thing she does . . .

Local sheriff Erick Harper wants Mitzy to have a loving remembrance of her mother. But after calling in a favor to get the dead woman's personal effects, he uncovers an unexpected skeleton hiding in the evidence. And now that the cat's out of the bag, he can't stop her from risking everything to dig up more clues.

Mitzy won't rest until she slams her mama's killer behind bars. And Erick is desperate to bring her back to Pin Cherry Harbor in one piece.

Can Mitzy deliver some Wild West justice, or will she bite the dust in the Arizona desert?

Tracks and Flashbacks is the ninth book in the hilarious paranormal cozy mystery series, Mitzy Moon Mysteries. If you like snarky heroines, supernatural intrigue, and a scoop of romance, then you'll love Trixie Silvertale's twisty whodunit.

Buy *Tracks and Flashbacks* to thaw out a cold case today!

***For loyal readers of the series, rest assured that Grams, Pye, and Silas will all make appearances in this "out of Pin Cherry" adventure!*

Grab yours here!
readerlinks.com/l/1313026

Once you're in the Club, you'll also be the first to receive updates from Pin Cherry Harbor and access to giveaways, new release announcements, behind-the-scenes secrets, and much more!

THANK YOU!

Trying out a new book is always a risk and I'm thankful that you rolled the dice with Mitzy Moon. If you loved the book, the sweetest thing you can do (*even sweeter than pin cherry pie à la mode*) is to leave a review so that other readers will take a chance on Mitzy and the gang.

Don't feel you have to write a book report. A brief comment like, "Can't wait to read the next book in this series!" will help potential readers make their choice.

★★★★★
Leave a quick review HERE
https://readerlinks.com/l/1157786
★★★★★

Thank you kindly, and I'll see you in Pin Cherry
Harbor!

ABOUT THE AUTHOR

Trixie Silvertale grew up reading an endless supply of Lilian Jackson Braun, Hardy Boys, and Nancy Drew novels. She loves the amateur sleuths in cozy mysteries and obsesses about all things paranormal. Those two passions unite in her Mitzy Moon Mysteries, and she's thrilled to write them and share them with you.

When she's not consumed by writing, she bakes to fuel her creative engine and pulls weeds in her herb garden to clear her head (*and sometimes she pulls out her hair, but mostly weeds*).

Greetings are welcome:
trixie@trixiesilvertale.com

BB bookbub.com/authors/trixie-silvertale

f facebook.com/TrixieSilvertale

O instagram.com/trixiesilvertale